UNITED NATIONS

UNITED
A Working Paper for Restructuring
NATIONS

by Harold Stassen

LERNER PUBLICATIONS COMPANY, MINNEAPOLIS, MINNESOTA USA

First published in 1994

The author gratefully acknowledges the financial assistance of
the Glenview Foundation of New York City, New York.

Copies of *United Nations: A Working Paper for Restructuring* can be
ordered from Lerner Publications Company, 241 First Avenue North,
Minneapolis, MN 55401, USA.

Library of Congress Cataloging-in-Publication Data

Stassen, Harold Edward, 1907–
   United Nations : a working paper for restructuring / by
Harold Stassen.
    p. cm.
   ISBN 0-8225-3149-6 (pbk.)
   1. United Nations. I. Title.
JX1977.S757 1994
341.23'2—dc20   93-47910
                                 CIP

Manufactured in the United States of America

1 2 3 4 5 6 · I/H · 99 98 97 96 95 94

In 1995
the Fiftieth Year

To Emerge from the Original Charter
and Better Serve All Peoples
for Peace and Progress
for the Next Half Century

CONTENTS

To represent the United States in 1945 at the San Francisco Conference, where the original United Nations Charter was hammered out, President Franklin Roosevelt appointed (left to right) Rep. Sol Bloom of New York; Dean Virginia Gildersleeve of Barnard College; Sen. Tom Connally of Texas; Secretary of State Edward R. Stettinius, Jr.; former Governor Harold Stassen of Minnesota; Sen. Arthur Vandenberg of Michigan; and Rep. Charles Eaton of New Jersey.

Governor Harold Stassen

PREFACE

With the ending of the cold war, the peoples of the world need the United Nations Organization today more than ever. The United Nations must become more effective in peacemaking, more efficient in peacekeeping, and more dynamic in securing the well-being of the children, women, and men of the world.

A rising tide of worldwide public opinion holds that the United Nations urgently needs to be restructured to accomplish these goals. I suggest that a restructuring be accomplished in the year 1995, the fiftieth year of the United Nations.

Such a restructuring should focus on two factors. First, the United Nations Organization of the future must effectively foster and develop the nonviolent and just inter-relationships of people of different religions, races, and ethnicities, within states and within bordering states. Second, the United Nations Organization of the future must become a world-changing, creative center, functioning effectively within the extremes of economic, political, social, religious, and philosophic thought.

To stimulate and encourage the process of restructuring, I have put together the "working paper" that follows, with my suggestions for revisions to the original United Nations Charter. In this working paper, I do not propose a world government. I do propose an improved center of cooperation between sovereign governments. It would include ten restructured institutions, as follows.

1. A regular annual conference at the United Nations of representative leaders of the religions of the world. The goal would be to find nonviolent and just solutions for future interrelationships of the peoples of the world. (Chapter XXIV, *A Working Paper*)

2. A small, elite, multilingual United Nations Legion of volunteers, with not too many from any one state or race or religion. The Legion should be well equipped and well trained to respond promptly to Security Council decisions regarding potential trouble spots. (Chapter VIII, *A Working Paper*)

3. A super peacemaking corps of experienced negotiators, mediators, and arbitrators to take long-term, continuing assignments to the most difficult international problems. (Chapters XIII and XIV, *A Working Paper*)

4. A Research Institute on People and Governance to study, suggest, and report on forms, methods, and revisions of national, regional, and international organizations, with special attention to future, worldwide conditions for health, economic opportunities, and human rights. (Chapter XXV, *A Working Paper*)

5. A continuation of a General Assembly of the United Nations, with every sovereign state Member having a voice and vote, but with voting power to be proportionate so that a more realistic, democratic, and sensible scale of voting rights can be achieved. (Chapter IV, *A Working Paper*)

6. An administrative council in the General Assembly to act continuously with the Secretary-General. The council would have regional representation and be of functional size (such as twenty-five members). It would foster regional cooperation, help defuse local conflicts, and improve world forums and administrative functioning. (Chapter VI, *A Working Paper*)

7. A new method of regular financial support, such as a small, one-half of one percent charge on all international trade of goods, materials, oil, and minerals. (Chapter XXIII, *A Working Paper*)

8. A Universe Environmental Institute to lift worldwide attention and scientific expertise regarding the quality of the water, air, and land of the globe. (Chapter VII, *A Working Paper*)

9. An effective inspection system and corps to monitor the continuing reduction of the offensive armaments of the world. (Chapter IX, *A Working Paper*)

10. A continuation of the Security Council, but with the addition of Japan and Germany as permanent Members (and perhaps one or two others), and with a revision of the single-member veto power. (Chapter V, *A Working Paper*)

Photo by UPI/Bettmann

The San Francisco Conference was one of the largest and perhaps most significant international gatherings ever held. Here Governor Harold Stassen sits amid other delegates at the opening meeting of the conference at the San Francisco Opera House in April 1945.

Britain's Earl of Halifax (left) *confers with U.S. delegates Virginia Gildersleeve and Harold Stassen at the United Nations Charter conference.*

Photo by UPI/Bettmann

The establishment of a restructured United Nations is a sound and urgent objective. Failure to restructure, in my view, would result in many adverse consequences for all of us. Such a failure could result in the rise of extreme, narrow nationalism of the type through which Hitler and the Nazi movement opened the disaster of World War II. It could result in the rise of the Tojo-type militarism that exploded in the Pearl Harbor attack of World War II. It could result in religious clashes of growing violence and hatred, and multiply regional trouble into world catastrophe. It could result in a gradual fading of the United Nations itself, as the League of Nations deteriorated after World War I, thus contributing to worldwide depression and to World War II.

When President Franklin Roosevelt died, the U.S. delegates to the San Francisco Conference were reappointed by President Harry Truman.

Together with President Truman, the U.S. delegates signed the original United Nations Charter, launching a new era of international cooperation.

Study and research programs—national and multinational, governmental and non-governmental—should be active in preparing for restructuring. "We the people," including many organizations and all of the world's religions, should be involved.

The suggestions in this working paper grow out of much reading, listening, and studying, and out of my observations of critical events and circumstances in our world. I recognize that there will be differences of opinion with many points; these can be resolved in the actual fulfillment of a restructuring.

For convenience in study, the following pages present the original United Nations Charter on the left; the working paper for a revised Charter appears on the right. Where the suggested revisions do not have a parallel in the original Charter, the left-hand page has been left blank. The suggestions have deliberately not been copyrighted, so that anyone is free to copy, with or without attribution, any of the ideas or language.

I do urge that "we the people" of the world persuade our governments now—with letters, editorials, resolutions, and sermons—to restructure the United Nations Organization, enabling it to better serve humankind for the next fifty years on this earth.

Harold Stassen

Note: The following pages present the original United Nations Charter on the left; the working paper for a revised Charter appears on the right. For convenience in comparing the two, chapters in the original Charter appear alongside corresponding chapters in the working paper, rather than in their original order. Where the suggested revisions do not have a parallel in the original Charter, the left-hand page has been left blank.

Preamble

WE THE PEOPLES OF THE UNITED NATIONS DETERMINED

to save succeeding generations from the scourge of war, which twice in our life-time has brought untold sorrow to mankind, and

to reaffirm faith in fundamental human rights, in the dignity and worth of the human person, in the equal rights of men and women and of nations large and small, and

to establish conditions under which justice and respect for the obligations arising from treaties and other sources of international law can be maintained, and

to promote social progress and better standards of life in larger freedom,

Preamble

WE THE PEOPLES OF THE UNITED NATIONS DETERMINED

to save our own and succeeding generations from the scourge of world war, which in this age of nuclear bombs and other weapons of mass destruction carries a catastrophic threat to all humanity;

to establish circumstances within which peoples of different races, varied religions, divergent ethnic origins, and a range of economic circumstances may live together in neighbor states and within individual states, without violence, and with mutual rights, justice, and progress;

to foster conditions under which the competition of systems—economic, social, and political—may take place without violence or war;

to encourage cooperative reaching out for common action for the mutual well-being of the world's peoples;

to care for this earth and safeguard the environment of the universe against hazardous pollution of air and water and land;

to establish methods and structures to consider all threats to peace and controversies between peoples and nations and to assist in reaching creative, sound, fair, and just solutions;

to advance standards of justice and fairness in world trade and economic development;

to decrease violent terrorism, which afflicts innocent children and women, as well as men, and in fact damages the future prospects of all peoples and increases the perils of war;

to end hunger, which is now a tragic experience of many peoples;

to overcome disease and illness that afflict humanity;

to extend humanitarian and expert aid in earthquakes, hurricanes, typhoons, volcanic eruptions, nuclear accidents, and other major disasters;

to advance the peaceful use of outer space for the well-being of humankind through Stars Peace and to decrease the danger of a future Star War;

to open the way for information, larger freedom, opportunity, and hope for the greater fulfillment and enjoyment of life for all of the children of all of the races of humankind;

to reaffirm faith in fundamental human rights, in the dignity and worth of the human person, in the equal rights of men and women, and in the equal rights of nations large and small, with respect for their sovereignty and their culture;

Determined to save our own and succeeding generations from the scourge of world war, to decrease violent terrorism, and to end hunger.

AND FOR THESE ENDS

to practice tolerance and live together in peace with one another as good neighbours, and
to unite our strength to maintain international peace and security, and
to ensure, by the acceptance of principles and the institution of methods, that armed force shall not be used, save in the common interest, and
to employ international machinery for the promotion of the economic and social advancement of all peoples,

HAVE RESOLVED TO COMBINE OUR EFFORTS TO ACCOMPLISH THESE AIMS

Accordingly, our respective Governments, through representatives assembled in the city of San Francisco, who have exhibited their full powers found to be in good and due form, have agreed to the present Charter of the United Nations and do hereby establish an international organization to be known as the United Nations.

AND FOR THESE ENDS

to practice tolerance, living together creatively and in peace with one another as good neighbors;
to unite our strength to maintain international peace and security;
to ensure, by the acceptance of principles and by the institution of methods, that armed forces shall not be used, save in the common interest; and
to employ, with wisdom, international organizations and methods to promote the economic, social, and cultural advance of all peoples;

HAVE RESOLVED TO COMBINE OUR EFFORTS TO ACCOMPLISH THESE ENDS

Accordingly, our respective governments, through representatives assembled, who have exhibited their full powers found to be in good and due form, have agreed to this Charter of the United Nations, to supersede upon its ratification, in accordance with the terms hereof, the previous Charter of the United Nations; and do hereby establish a renewed international organization to be known as the United Nations.

To practice tolerance and live together creatively in peace with one another as good neighbors; to unite our strength to maintain international peace and security; and to employ, with wisdom, international organizations to promote the economic, social, and cultural advance of all peoples.

Chapter I
PURPOSES AND PRINCIPLES

Article 1

The Purposes of the United Nations are:

1. To maintain international peace and security, and to that end: to take effective collective measures for the prevention and removal of threats to the peace, and for the suppression of acts of aggression or other breaches of the peace, and to bring about by peaceful means, and in conformity with the principles of justice and international law, adjustment or settlement of international disputes or situations which might lead to a breach of the peace;

2. To develop friendly relations among nations based on respect for the principle of equal rights and self-determination of peoples, and to take other appropriate measures to strengthen universal peace;

3. To achieve international cooperation in solving international problems of an economic, social, cultural, or humanitarian character, and in promoting and encouraging respect for human rights and for fundamental freedoms for all without distinction as to race, sex, language, or religion; and

4. To be a centre for harmonizing the actions of nations in the attainment of these common ends.

Chapter I
PURPOSES AND PRINCIPLES

Article 1

The purposes of the United Nations are:

1. To maintain international peace and security, and to that end to take effective collective measures: for preventing and removing threats to the peace; for suppressing acts of aggression or terrorism or other breaches to the peace; for stopping the arms race; for reducing armaments reciprocally; and for bringing about by peaceful means, and in conformity with the principles of justice and international law, adjustment or settlement of international disputes or situations that might lead to a breach of the peace;

2. To establish conditions under which the competition of systems—economic, social, cultural, and political—can take place without resort to violence, terrorism, or war, and which facilitate common action for the mutual well-being of all peoples;

3. To care for this earth and to establish safeguards for the environment of the universe against the hazardous pollution of air and water and land;

4. To develop friendly relations among nations based on respect for the principle of equal rights and self-determination of peoples, and to take appropriate measures to strengthen universal peace;

5. To achieve international cooperation in solving international problems of an economic, social, cultural, or humanitarian character, and in promoting and encouraging respect for human rights and for fundamental freedoms for all men, women, and children, without distinction as to race, language, or religion;

6. To administer those areas of this earth and of the space around this earth that are not within the sovereign jurisdiction of any state;

7. To be a center for harmonizing the actions of nations in the attainment of these common ends.

To establish conditions under which the competition of systems, economic, social, cultural, and political, may take place without violence.

Article 2

The Organization and its Members, in pursuit of the Purposes stated in Article 1, shall act in accordance with the following Principles.

1. The Organization is based on the principle of the sovereign equality of all its Members.

2. All Members, in order to ensure to all of them the rights and benefits resulting from membership, shall fulfil in good faith the obligations assumed by them in accordance with the present Charter.

3. All Members shall settle their international disputes by peaceful means in such a manner that international peace and security, and justice, are not endangered.

4. All Members shall refrain in their international relations from the threat or use of force against the territorial integrity or political independence of any state, or in any other manner inconsistent with the Purposes of the United Nations.

5. All Members shall give the United Nations every assistance in any action it takes in accordance with the present Charter, and shall refrain from giving assistance to any state against which the United Nations is taking preventive or enforcement action.

6. The Organization shall ensure that states which are not Members of the United Nations act in accordance with these Principles so far as may be necessary for the maintenance of international peace and security.

7. Nothing contained in the present Charter shall authorize the United Nations to intervene in matters which are essentially within the domestic jurisdiction of any state or shall require the Members to submit such matters to settlement under the present Charter; but this principle shall not prejudice the application of enforcement measures under Chapter VII.

Article 2

The United Nations Organization and its Members, in pursuit of the purposes stated in Article 1, shall act in accordance with the following principles:

1. The Organization is based on the principle of the sovereign equality of all its Members, and of universally encompassing within it the contemporary governments of all peoples on this earth.

2. All Members, in order to ensure to all of them the rights and benefits resulting from membership, shall fulfill in good faith the obligations assumed by them in accordance with this Charter.

3. All Members shall settle their international disputes by peaceful means in such a manner that international peace and security are not endangered and justice may be attained.

4. All Members shall refrain in their international relations from the threat or use of force against the territorial integrity or political independence of any state, or in any other manner inconsistent with the purposes of the United Nations.

5. No Member that possesses nuclear weapons shall ever use such weapons against a Member that is not engaged in massive military aggression, and all such Members shall open their territories to reasonable United Nations inspection to assure the fulfillment of this commitment.

6. No Member shall send nuclear weapons into space, and all Members shall permit United Nations inspectors to assure the absence of nuclear weapons before the launching of any object into space.

7. All Members shall give the United Nations assistance in accordance with this Charter, and shall refrain from giving assistance to any state against which the United Nations is taking preventive enforcement action.

8. The Organization shall ensure that states which are not Members of the United Nations act in accordance with these Principles so far as may be necessary for the maintenance of international peace and security.

9. Nothing contained in this Charter shall authorize the United Nations to intervene in matters that are essentially within the domestic jurisdiction of any state or shall require the Members to submit such matters to settlement under this Charter; but this principle shall not prejudice the application of enforcement measures under Chapter IX.

The Organization is based on the principle of the sovereign equality of all its Members.

Chapter II
MEMBERSHIP

Article 3

The original Members of the United Nations shall be the states which, having participated in the United Nations Conference on International Organization at San Francisco, or having previously signed the Declaration of United Nations by 1 January 1942, sign the present Charter and ratify it in accordance with Article 10.

Article 4

1. Membership in the United Nations is open to all other peace-loving states which accept the obligations contained in the present Charter and, in the judgment of the Organization, are able and willing to carry out these obligations.

2. The admission of any such state to membership in the United Nations will be effected by a decision of the General Assembly upon the recommendation of the Security Council.

Article 5

A Member of the United Nations against which preventive or enforcement action has been taken by the Security Council may be suspended from the exercise of the rights and privileges of membership by the General Assembly upon the recommendation of the Security Council. The exercise of these rights and privileges may be restored by the Security Council.

Article 6

A Member of the United Nations which has persistently violated the Principles contained in the present Charter may be expelled from the Organization by the General Assembly upon the recommendation of the Security Council.

Chapter II
MEMBERSHIP

Article 3

The original Members of the United Nations under this Charter shall be the states which sign this Charter and ratify it in accordance with Article 184 within one year of the date on which the minimum requirements for ratification are completed for the effective enactment of this Charter.

Article 4

1. Membership in the United Nations is open universally to all states, the effective governments of which accept the obligations contained in this Charter.

2. The admission of any such state to Membership in the United Nations after the original Members will be effected by a decision of the General Assembly, with the concurrence of the Central Cabinet of Administrators.

3. Membership in the United Nations, through such acceptance of the obligations contained in this Charter by the effective government of any state, shall not constitute approval of such government by the United Nations, or by the Member states, or of either the form or the personnel or the practices of such government.

Article 5

A Member of the United Nations against which preventive or enforcement action has been taken by the Security Council may be suspended from the exercise of the rights and privileges of membership by the General Assembly upon the recommendation of the Security Council. The exercise of these rights and privileges may be restored by the Security Council.

Article 6

A Member of the United Nations that has persistently violated the Principles contained in this Charter may be suspended from the Organization by the General Assembly upon the recommendation of the Central Council of Administrators or of the Security Council.

Membership in the United Nations is open universally to all states.

Chapter III
ORGANS

Article 7

1. There are established as the principal organs of the United Nations: a General Assembly, a Security Council, an Economic and Social Council, a Trusteeship Council, an International Court of Justice, and a Secretariat.

2. Such subsidiary organs as may be found necessary may be established in accordance with the present Charter.

Article 8

The United Nations shall place no restrictions on the eligibility of men and women to participate in any capacity and under conditions of equality in its principal and subsidiary organs.

Chapter III
INSTITUTIONS

Article 7

1. There are established as the principal institutions of the United Nations: a General Assembly, a Security Council, a Central Cabinet of Administrators, a Universe Environmental Institute, a United Nations Legion, an Inspection Corps, an Economic and Social Council, a Trusteeship Council, an International Court of Justice, a World Court of Equity, a World Board of Arbitration, a World Panel of Mediators, a Worldwide Conference of Religions, a Research Institute of People and Governance, and a Secretariat.

2. Such subsidiary organs as may be found necessary may be established in accordance with this Charter. Subsidiary organs established under the original Charter shall be continued under this Charter.

Article 8

The United Nations shall place no discriminating restrictions on the eligibility of men and women of all races to participate in any capacity and under conditions of equality in its principal and subsidiary organs.

There are established a Universe Environmental Institute and a Worldwide Conference of Religions.

Chapter IV
THE GENERAL ASSEMBLY

Composition

Article 9

1. The General Assembly shall consist of all the Members of the United Nations.

2. Each Member shall have not more than five representatives in the General Assembly.

Functions and Powers

Article 10

The General Assembly may discuss any questions or any matters within the scope of the present Charter or relating to the powers and functions of any organs provided for in the present Charter, and, except as provided in Article 12, may make recommendations to the Members of the United Nations or to the Security Council or to both on any such questions or matters.

Article 11

1. The General Assembly may consider the general principles of cooperation in the maintenance of international peace and security, including the principles governing disarmament and the regulation of armaments, and may make recommendations with regard to such principles to the Members or to the Security Council or to both.

2. The General Assembly may discuss any questions relating to the maintenance of international peace and security brought before it by any Member of the United Nations, or by the Security Council, or by a state which is not a member of the United Nations in accordance with Article 35, paragraph 2, and, except as provided in Article 12, may make recommendations with regard to any such questions to the state or states concerned or to the Security Council or to both.

Chapter IV
THE GENERAL ASSEMBLY

Composition

Article 9

1. The General Assembly shall consist of all the Members of the United Nations.

2. Each Member shall have not more than three representatives in the General Assembly, and each member shall have equal rights to speak and express views in the sessions of the Assembly, and in all activities and forums of the Assembly.

3. Each member shall have the voting rights established by Article 18.

*E*ach Member shall have equal rights to speak.

Functions and Powers

Article 10

The General Assembly may discuss any questions or any matters within the scope of the present Charter or relating to the powers and functions of any organization provided for in this Charter, and, except as provided in Article 12, may make recommendations to the Members of the United Nations or to any of the other institutions of the United Nations, or to both, on any such questions or matters.

Article 11

1. The General Assembly may consider the general principles of cooperation in the maintenance of international peace and security, including the principles governing disarmament and the regulation of armaments, and may make recommendations with regard to such principles to the Members or to the Security Council or to both.

2. The General Assembly may discuss any questions relating to the maintenance of international peace and security brought before it by any Member of the United Nations, or by the Security Council, or by the Central Cabinet of Administrators, or by a state that is not a Member of the United Nations in accordance with Article

Any such questions on which action is necessary shall be referred to the Security Council by the General Assembly either before or after discussion.

3. The General Assembly may call the attention of the Security Council to situations which are likely to endanger international peace and security.

4. The powers of the General Assembly set forth in this Article shall not limit the general scope of Article 10.

Article 12

1. While the Security Council is exercising in respect of any dispute or situation the functions assigned to it in the present Charter, the General Assembly shall not make any recommendation with regard to that dispute or situation unless the Security Council so requests.

2. The Secretary-General, with the consent of the Security Council, shall notify the General Assembly at each session of any matters relative to the maintenance of international peace and security which are being dealt with by the Security Council and shall similarly notify the General Assembly, or the Members of the United Nations if the General Assembly is not in session, immediately if the Security Council ceases to deal with such matters.

Article 13

1. The General Assembly shall initiate studies and make recommendations for the purpose of:

a. promoting international cooperation in the political field and encouraging the progressive development of international law and its codification;

b. promoting international cooperation in the economic, social, cultural, educational, and health fields, and assisting in the realization of human rights and fundamental freedoms for all without distinction as to race, sex, language, or religion.

116 and except as provided in Article 24, may make recommendations with regard to any such questions to the state or states concerned or to the Security Council or to both. Any such questions on which action is necessary shall be referred to the Security Council by the General Assembly either before or after discussion.

3. The General Assembly may call the attention of the Security Council and the Central Cabinet of Administrators to situations likely to endanger international peace and security.

4. The powers of the General Assembly set forth in this Article shall not limit the general scope of Article 10.

Article 12

1. While the Security Council is exercising in respect of any dispute or situation the functions assigned to it in this Charter, the General Assembly shall not make any recommendations with regard to that dispute or situation unless the Security Council so requests.

2. The Secretary-General, with the consent of the Security Council, shall notify the General Assembly at each session of any matters relative to the maintenance of international peace and security that are being dealt with by the Security Council and shall similarly notify the General Assembly, or the Members of the United Nations if the General Assembly is not in session, immediately if the Security Council ceases to deal with such matters.

Article 13

1. The General Assembly shall initiate studies and make recommendations for the purpose of:

(a) promoting international cooperation in the political field and encouraging the progressive development of international law and its codification;

(b) promoting international cooperation in the economic, social, cultural, educational, and health fields, and assisting in the realization of human rights and fundamental freedoms for all without distinction as to race, sex, language, or religion;

The General Assembly may call the attention of the Security Council and the Central Cabinet of Administrators to situations that are likely to endanger international peace and security.

2. The further responsibilities, functions and powers of the General Assembly with respect to matters mentioned in paragraph 1(b) above are set forth in Chapters IX and X.

Article 14

Subject to the provisions of Article 12, the General Assembly may recommend measures for the peaceful adjustment of any situation, regardless of origin, which it deems likely to impair the general welfare or friendly relations among nations, including situations resulting from a violation of the provisions of the present Charter setting forth the Purposes and Principles of the United Nations.

Article 15

1. The General Assembly shall receive and consider the annual and special reports from the Security Council; these reports shall include an account of the measures that the Security Council has decided upon or taken to maintain international peace and security.

2. The General Assembly shall receive and consider reports from the other organs of the United Nations.

Article 16

The General Assembly shall perform such functions with respect to the international trusteeship system as are assigned to it under Chapters XII and XIII, including the approval of the trusteeship agreements for areas not designated as strategic.

Article 17

1. The General Assembly shall consider and approve the budget of the Organization.

2. The expenses of the Organization shall be borne by the Members as apportioned by the General Assembly.

3. The General Assembly shall consider and approve any financial and budgetary arrangements with specialized agencies referred to in Article 57 and shall examine the administrative budgets of such specialized agencies with a view to making recommendations to the agencies concerned.

(c) safeguarding the environment of the earth and of the universe and preventing the deepening pollution of the air, the water, and the land;

(d) developing the resources of the seas and of space and of areas outside of the sovereign jurisdiction of the separate states.

Article 14

Subject to the provisions of Article 24, the General Assembly may recommend measures for the peaceful adjustment of any situation, regardless of origin, which it deems likely to impair the general welfare or friendly relations among nations, including situations resulting from a violation of the provisions of this Charter setting forth the purposes and principles of the United Nations.

Article 15

The General Assembly may provide for an annual "We the People" assembly of accredited nongovernmental organizations that manifest a constructive interest in the purposes of the United Nations Charter.

Article 16

The General Assembly shall perform such functions with respect to the international trusteeship as are assigned to it under Chapter XX and Chapter XXI, including the approval of the trusteeship agreements for areas not designated as strategic.

Article 17

The General Assembly shall receive and consider an annual report from the Central Cabinet of Administrators, and such special reports as may be made.

Promoting international cooperation in the economic, social, cultural, educational, and health fields.

Voting

Article 18

1. Each member of the General Assembly shall have one vote.

2. Decisions of the General Assembly on important questions shall be made by a two-thirds majority of the members present and voting. These questions shall include: recommendations with respect to the maintenance of international peace and security, the election of the non-permanent members of the Security Council, the election of the members of the Economic and Social Council, the election of members of the Trusteeship Council in accordance with paragraph 1(c) of Article 86, the admission of new Members to the United Nations, the suspension of the rights and privileges of membership, the expulsion of Members, questions relating to the operation of the trusteeship system, and budgetary questions.

3. Decisions on other questions, including the determination of additional categories of questions to be decided by a two-thirds majority, shall be made by a majority of the members present and voting.

Voting

Article 18

1. Each Member of the General Assembly shall have not less than one vote and not more than four hundred votes. The specific number of votes of each member shall be established by taking into equal account three factors:

(a) total population

(b) annual gross national production

(c) annual per capita production.

All members shall be ranked on these three factors, and the three rankings shall be combined to establish the effective rankings. The initial voting rights are to be negotiated and added to this Charter. Thereafter, rankings shall be reviewed and raised or lowered each five years on the basis of the best available statistics for the comparative three-year period, by decisions of the Assembly.

2. Decisions of the General Assembly on important questions shall be made by a two-thirds majority of the votes of the Members present and voting. These questions shall include: recommendations with respect to the maintenance of international peace and security, the election of the nonpermanent Members of the Security Council, the election of the Members of the Economic and Social Council, the election of the Members of the Trusteeship Council in accordance with Article 77, the admission of new Members to the United Nations, the suspension of the rights and privileges of membership, questions relating to the operation of the trusteeship system, and budgetary questions.

3. Decisions on other questions, including the determination of additional categories of questions to be decided by a two-thirds majority, shall be made by a majority of the votes of Members present and voting.

Each Member shall have not less than one vote and not more than four hundred votes.

Article 19

A Member of the United Nations which is in arrears in the payment of its financial contributions to the Organization shall have no vote in the General Assembly if the amount of its arrears equals or exceeds the amount of the contributions due from it for the preceding two full years. The General Assembly may, nevertheless, permit such a Member to vote if it is satisfied that the failure to pay is due to conditions beyond the control of the Member.

Procedure

Article 20

The General Assembly shall meet in regular annual session and in such special sessions as occasion may require. Special sessions shall be convoked by the Secretary-General at the request of the Security Council or of a majority of the Members of the United Nations.

Article 21

The General Assembly shall adopt its own rules of procedure. It shall elect its President for each session.

Article 22

The General Assembly may establish such subsidiary organs as it deems necessary for the performance of its functions.

Article 19

A Member of the United Nations that is in arrears in the payment of its financial contributions to the Organization shall have no vote in the General Assembly if the amount of its arrears equals or exceeds the amount of the contributions due from it for the preceding two full years. The General Assembly may, nevertheless, permit such a Member to vote if it is satisfied that the failure to pay is due to conditions beyond the control of the Member.

Procedure

Article 20

The General Assembly shall meet in regular annual sessions and in such special sessions as occasion may require. Special sessions shall be convoked by the Secretary-General at the request of the Security Council or of a majority of the Members of the United Nations.

Article 21

The General Assembly shall adopt its own rules of procedure. It shall elect its President for each session.

Article 22

The General Assembly may establish such subsidiary organs as it deems necessary for the performance of its functions.

The General Assembly shall adopt its own rules of procedures.

Chapter V

THE SECURITY COUNCIL

Composition

Article 23

1. The Security Council shall consist of fifteen Members of the United Nations. The Republic of China, France, the Union of Soviet Socialist Republics, the United Kingdom of Great Britain and Northern Ireland, and the United States of America shall be permanent members of the Security Council. The General Assembly shall elect ten other Members of the United Nations to be non-permanent members of the Security Council, due regard being specially paid, in the first instance to the contribution of Members of the United Nations to the maintenance of international peace and security and to the other purposes of the Organization, and also to equitable geographical distribution.

2. The non-permanent members of the Security Council shall be elected for a term of two years. In the first election of the non-permanent members after the increase of the membership of the Security Council from eleven to fifteen, two of the four additional members shall be chosen for a term of one year. A retiring member shall not be eligible for immediate re-election.

3. Each member of the Security Council shall have one representative.

Chapter V
THE SECURITY COUNCIL

Composition

Article 23

1. The Security Council shall consist of twenty-one Members of the United Nations. The People's Republic of China, France, Germany, Japan, Russia, the United Kingdom of Great Britain and Northern Ireland, and the United States of America, or such of these states as are Members of the United Nations, shall be permanent Members of the Security Council. Of these permanent Members, the United States of America and Russia shall be special permanent Members. The General Assembly, acting with the voting rights provided in Article 18, shall elect additional Members of the Security Council to bring the total number to twenty-one, due regard being specially paid to the contribution of Members of the United Nations to the maintenance of international peace and security and to the other purposes of the Organization, and also to equitable geographical distribution.

2. The nonpermanent Members of the Security Council shall be elected for a term of two years. In the first election of the nonpermanent Members, however, one-half shall be chosen for a term of one year. A retiring Member shall not be eligible for immediate reelection.

3. Each Member of the Security Council shall have one representative.

The Security Council shall consist of twenty-one Members of the United Nations.

Functions and Powers

Article 24

1. In order to ensure prompt and effective action by the United Nations, its Members confer on the Security Council primary responsibility for the maintenance of international peace and security, and agree that in carrying out its duties under this responsibility the Security Council acts on their behalf.

2. In discharging these duties the Security Council shall act in accordance with the Purposes and Principles of the United Nations. The specific powers granted to the Security Council for the discharge of these duties are laid down in Chapters VI, VII, VIII, and XII.

3. The Security Council shall submit annual and, when necessary, special reports to the General Assembly for its consideration.

Article 25

The Members of the United Nations agree to accept and carry out the decisions of the Security Council in accordance with the present Charter.

Article 26

In order to promote the establishment and maintenance of international peace and security with the least diversion for armaments of the world's human and economic resources, the Security Council shall be responsible for formulating, with the assistance of the Military Staff Committee referred to in Article 47, plans to be submitted to the Members of the United Nations for the establishment of a system for the regulation of armaments.

Voting

Article 27

1. Each member of the Security Council shall have one vote.

2. Decisions of the Security Council on procedural matters shall be made by an affirmative vote of nine members.

3. Decisions of the Security Council on all other matters shall be made by an affirmative vote of nine members including the concurring votes of the permanent members; provided that, in decisions under Chapter VI, and under paragraph 3 of Article 52, a party to a dispute shall abstain from voting.

Function and Powers

Article 24

1. In order to ensure prompt and effective action by the United Nations, its Members confer on the Security Council primary responsibility for the maintenance of international peace and security, and agree that in carrying out its duties under this responsibility the Security Council acts on their behalf.

2. In discharging these duties the Security Council shall act in accordance with the purposes and principles of the United Nations. The specific powers granted to the Security Council for the discharge of these duties are laid down in Chapters V, XVII, and XVIII.

3. The Security Council shall submit annual and, when necessary, special reports to the General Assembly for its consideration.

Article 25

The Members of the United Nations agree to accept and carry out the decisions of the Security Council in accordance with this Charter.

Article 26

In order to promote the establishment and maintenance of international peace and security with the least diversion for armaments of the world's human and economic resources, the Security Council shall be responsible for formulating plans to be submitted to the Members of the United Nations for the establishment of a system for the regulation and limitation of armaments.

Voting

Article 27

1. Each Member of the Security Council shall have one vote.

2. Decisions of the Security Council on procedural matters shall be made by an affirmative vote of twelve or more Members.

3. Decisions of the Security Council on all matters that include the use of military force by the United Nations, or the approval of the use of military force by a member of the United Nations, shall be made by an affirmative vote of twelve Members, including the concurring votes of the special permanent Members and the concurring vote of three-fourths of the permanent Members.

4. Decisions of the Security Council on all other matters shall be made by a concurring vote of two-thirds of the permanent Members and by the affirmative vote of fourteen or more Members.

Members confer on the Security Council primary responsibility for the maintenance of international peace and security.

Procedure

Article 28

1. The Security Council shall be so organized as to be able to function continuously. Each member of the Security Council shall for this purpose be represented at all times at the seat of the Organization.

2. The Security Council shall hold periodic meetings at which each of its members may, if it so desires, be represented by a member of the government or by some other specially designated representative.

3. The Security Council may hold meetings at such places other than the seat of the Organization as in its judgment will best facilitate its work.

Article 29

The Security Council may establish such subsidiary organs as it deems necessary for the performance of its functions.

Article 30

The Security Council shall adopt its own rules of procedure, including the method of selecting its President.

Article 31

Any Member of the United Nations which is not a member of the Security Council may participate, without vote, in the discussion of any question brought before the Security Council whenever the latter considers that the interests of that Member are specially affected.

Article 32

Any Member of the United Nations which is not a member of the Security Council or any state which is not a Member of the United Nations, if it is a party to a dispute under consideration by the Security Council, shall be invited to participate, without vote, in the discussion relating to the dispute. The Security Council shall lay down such conditions as it deems just for the participation of a state which is not a Member of the United Nations.

Procedure

Article 28

1. The Security Council shall be so organized as to be able to function continuously. Each Member of the Security Council shall for this purpose be represented at all times at the seat of the Organization.

2. The Security Council shall hold periodic meetings at which each of its Members may, if it so desires, be represented by a Member of the government or by some other specially designated representative.

3. The Security Council may hold meetings at such places other than the seat of the Organization as in its judgment will best facilitate its work.

Article 29

The Security Council may establish such subsidiary organs as it deems necessary for the performance of its functions.

Article 30

The Security Council shall adopt its own rules of procedure, including the method of selecting its President.

Article 31

Any Member of the United Nations that is not a Member of the Security Council may participate, without vote, in the discussion of any question brought before the Security Council whenever the latter considers that the interests of that Member are specially affected.

Article 32

Any Member of the United Nations that is not a Member of the Security Council, or any state that is not a Member of the United Nations, if it is a party to a dispute under consideration by the Security Council, shall be invited to participate, without vote, in the discussion relating to the dispute. The Security Council shall lay down such conditions as it deems just for the participation of a state that is not a Member of the United Nations.

The Security Council shall be so organized as to be able to function continuously.

NOTE—No parallel provisions
in the original 1945
United Nations Charter

Chapter VI
THE CENTRAL CABINET OF ADMINISTRATORS

Article 33

The Central Cabinet of Administrators shall consist of twenty-five Administrators each appointed by and representing one Member state or a group of Member states.

Article 34

The appointment of Administrators to represent groups of Member states shall be by the application of the respective voting rights of the Member states within the region.

Article 35

The Administrators shall vote within the Central Cabinet of Administrators by the application of the voting rights of the Member state or group of Member states within the region represented by the Administrator.

Article 36

The appointment of Administrators shall be for a term of five years. Vacancies shall be filled for an unexpired term. An Administrator may be removed from office and a successor appointed at any time by the majority voting rights of the Member states of the region.

Article 37

The Secretary-General shall serve as Chairman of the Central Cabinet of Administrators. In the absence of the Secretary-General, the Central Cabinet of Administrators shall select a Chairman from its own membership.

The Central Cabinet of Administrators shall consist of twenty-five Administrators.

NOTE—No parallel provisions
in the original 1945
United Nations Charter

Article 38

Each Administrator shall appoint a deputy Administrator and a second deputy Administrator who shall serve as alternates respectively with full power in meetings of the Central Cabinet in the absence of the Administrators. Proxies shall not be permitted.

Article 39

The Central Cabinet of Administrators will have primary authority and responsibility on behalf of the United Nations in matters of the oceans, ocean beds, and outer space, beyond the jurisdiction of individual Member states.

Article 40

The Central Cabinet of Administrators may make recommendations upon any matter within the scope of the Charter, but may not supersede or interfere with the functioning of any other organ of the United Nations.

Article 41

The Central Cabinet of Administrators shall meet regularly at least twice a month at the headquarters of the United Nations.

Article 42

Each Administrator shall maintain an office at the headquarters of the United Nations.

Article 43

The Central Cabinet of Administrators shall establish, approve, and administer the budget of the United Nations.

The Central Cabinet of Administrators will have primary authority in matters of the oceans, ocean beds, and outer space.

NOTE—No parallel provisions
in the original 1945
United Nations Charter

Chapter VII
UNIVERSE ENVIRONMENTAL INSTITUTE

Article 44

A Universe Environmental Institute is established.

Article 45

Each member state may appoint one Scientist-Representative to the Universe Environmental Council.

Article 46

The Universe Environmental Institute shall hold an annual scientific conference at which reports of research on matters affecting the environment of the universe may be presented.

A Universe Environmental Institute is established.

Article 47

The Universe Environmental Institute shall not have authority to issue any orders or directives or requirements to any member state.

Article 48

The Universe Environmental Institute shall have the authority to issue and publish recommendations to member states, including the authority to draft suggested treaties for consideration by member states.

Article 49

The Secretary-General shall appoint, with the approval of two-thirds of the Scientist-Representatives, a Director-Administrator of the Universe Environmental Institute.

Article 50

The budget of the Universe Environmental Institute shall be approved by the Central Cabinet of Administrators.

NOTE—No parallel provisions
in the original 1945
United Nations Charter

Chapter VIII
THE UNITED NATIONS LEGION

Article 52

A United Nations Legion shall be established by the United Nations to serve as a police and peace force.

Article 53

The United Nations Legion shall consist of not more than 250,000 individuals.

Article 54

The United Nations Legion shall consist exclusively of volunteers for service in the force for a term of not less than five years.

Article 55

Not more than ten percent of the number of the United Nations Legion in being at any one time may be citizens of any one Member state, and none shall be citizens of a special permanent Member of the Security Council.

Article 56

The United Nations Legion shall be highly trained, well equipped, multilingual, and prepared for the four special purposes of acting:

1. as a buffer in tense situations which are a threat to peace;

2. as a stabilizing or security force in conjunction with the functioning of any United Nations commission or organization;

3. to decrease violent terrorism upon the peoples of the world; and

4. to interdict the international movement of addicting drugs and chemical substances hazardous to humankind.

A United Nations Legion shall be established to serve as a police and peace force.

NOTE—No parallel provisions
in the original 1945
United Nations Charter

Article 57

The commanders of the United Nations Legion, and of each special task force formed by the United Nations Legion, shall be appointed by the Secretary-General and shall be citizens of Member states that are not special permanent Members of the Security Council.

Article 58

The United Nations Legion shall have a uniform that is distinctive from the uniform of Member states and that is exclusive. Member states are not to copy the uniform of the United Nations Legion.

Article 59

All Member states, except the special permanent Members of the Security Council, agree to permit individual citizens to serve in such a United Nations Legion if they volunteer and if they are accepted for the purpose, and to safeguard and respect all such volunteers' rights within their states during and after such service without discrimination.

Article 60

The United Nations Legion shall serve exclusively in accordance with assignments and directions received from the Security Council.

All Member states agree to permit individual citizens to serve in such a United Nations Legion.

NOTE—No parallel provisions
in the original 1945
United Nations Charter

Chapter IX
INSPECTION CORPS

Article 61

An Inspection Corps is hereby established in the United Nations. This Inspection Corps shall have the responsibility, the personnel, and the modern equipment to fulfill the inspecting, monitoring, and safeguarding assignments of the United Nations, to give maximum assurance of an open and peaceful world.

Article 62

The personnel of the Inspection Corps shall be recruited voluntarily, shall not include any nationals of the two special permanent Members of the Security Council, and shall not include more than five percent in number of the nationals of any Member of the United Nations.

Article 63

The special permanent Members of the Security Council shall be entitled to have accredited observers at each inspection post, and at each inspection installation, and at all inspection headquarters, with access to all reports, and with facilities for communication with their respective governments.

Article 64

The Inspection Corps shall be under the management of a Director, who shall be a national of a Member state, and who shall not be a national of a special permanent Member of the Security Council. The Director shall be appointed by a majority vote of the Central Cabinet of Administrators, with the approval of the special permanent Members of the Security Council.

A n Inspection Corps is hereby established to give maximum assurance of an open, peaceful world.

Chapter X
THE ECONOMIC AND SOCIAL COUNCIL

Composition

Article 61

1. The Economic and Social Council shall consist of fifty-four Members of the United Nations elected by the General Assembly.

2. Subject to the provisions of paragraph 3, eighteen members of the Economic and Social Council shall be elected each year for a term of three years. A retiring member shall be eligible for immediate re-election.

3. At the first election after the increase in the membership of the Economic and Social Council from twenty-seven to fifty-four members, in addition to the members elected in place of the nine members whose term of office expires at the end of that year, twenty-seven additional members shall be elected. Of these twenty-seven additional members, the term of office of nine members so elected shall expire at the end of one year, and of nine other members at the end of two years, in accordance with arrangements made by the General Assembly.

4. Each member of the Economic and Social Council shall have one representative.

Functions and Powers

Article 62

1. The Economic and Social Council may make or initiate studies and reports with respect to international economic, social, cultural, educational, health, and related matters and may make recommendations with respect to any such matters to the General Assembly, to the Members of the United Nations, and to the specialized agencies concerned.

2. It may make recommendations for the purpose of promoting respect for, and observance of, human rights and fundamental freedoms for all.

3. It may prepare draft conventions for submission to the General Assembly, with respect to matters falling within its competence.

4. It may call, in accordance with the rules prescribed by the United Nations, international conferences on matters falling within its competence.

Chapter X
THE ECONOMIC AND SOCIAL COUNCIL

Composition

Article 65

1. The Economic and Social Council shall consist of twenty-seven Members of the United Nations elected by the General Assembly.

2. Subject to the provisions of Paragraph 3, nine Members of the Economic and Social Council shall be elected each year for a term of three years. A retiring Member shall be eligible for immediate reelection.

3. At the first election, twenty-seven Members of the Economic and Social Council shall be chosen. The term of office of nine Members so chosen shall expire at the end of one year, and of nine other Members at the end of two years, in accordance with arrangements made by the General Assembly.

4. Each Member of the Economic and Social Council shall have one representative.

Functions and Powers

Article 66

1. The Economic and Social Council may make or initiate studies and reports with respect to international economic, social, cultural, educational, health, and related matters and may make recommendations with respect to any such matters to the General Assembly, to the Members of the Central Cabinet of Administrators, to the Members of the United Nations, and to the specialized agencies concerned.

2. The Economic and Social Council may make recommendations for the purpose of promoting respect for, and observance of, human rights and fundamental freedoms for all.

3. The Economic and Social Council may prepare draft conventions for submission to the General Assembly with respect to matters falling within its competence.

4. The Economic and Social Council may call, in accordance with the rules prescribed by the United Nations, international conferences on matters falling within its competence.

The Economic and Social Council may make recommendations for promoting respect for, and observance of, human rights and fundamental freedoms for all.

Article 63

1. The Economic and Social Council may enter into agreements with any of the agencies referred to in Article 57, defining the terms on which the agency concerned shall be brought into relationship with the United Nations. Such agreements shall be subject to approval by the General Assembly.

2. It may co-ordinate the activities of the specialized agencies through consultation with and recommendations to such agencies and through recommendations to the General Assembly and to the Members of the United Nations.

Article 64

1. The Economic and Social Council may take appropriate steps to obtain regular reports from the specialized agencies. It may make arrangements with the Members of the United Nations and with the specialized agencies to obtain reports on the steps taken to give effect to its own recommendations and to recommendations on matters falling within its competence made by the General Assembly.

2. It may communicate its observations on these reports to the General Assembly.

Article 65

The Economic and Social Council may furnish information to the Security Council and shall assist the Security Council upon its request.

Article 66

1. The Economic and Social Council shall perform such functions as fall within its competence in connexion with the carrying out of the recommendations of the General Assembly.

2. It may, with the approval of the General Assembly, perform services at the request of Members of the United Nations and at the request of specialized agencies.

3. It shall perform such other functions as are specified elsewhere in the present Charter or as may be assigned to it by the General Assembly.

Article 67

1. The Economic and Social Council may enter into agreements with any of the agencies referred to in Article 133, defining the terms on which the agency concerned shall be brought into relationship with the United Nations. Such agreements shall be subject to approval by the General Assembly.

2. The Economic and Social Council may coordinate the activities of the specialized agencies through consultation with and recommendations to such agencies and through recommendations to the General Assembly and to the Members of the United Nations.

Article 68

1. The Economic and Social Council may take appropriate steps to obtain regular reports from the specialized agencies. It may make arrangements with the Members of the United Nations and with the specialized agencies to obtain reports on the steps taken to give effect to its own recommendations on matters falling within its competence made by the General Assembly.

Article 69

The Economic and Social Council may furnish information to the Security Council and shall assist the Security Council upon its request.

Article 70

1. The Economic and Social Council shall perform such functions as fall within its competence in connection with the carrying out of the recommendations of the General Assembly.

2. The Economic and Social Council may, with the approval of the General Assembly, perform services at the request of Members of the United Nations and at the request of specialized agencies.

3. The Economic and Social Council shall perform such other functions as are specified elsewhere in this Charter or as may be assigned to it by the General Assembly.

The Economic and Social Council may coordinate the activities of the specialized agencies.

Voting

Article 67

1. Each member of the Economic and Social Council shall have one vote.

2. Decisions of the Economic and Social Council shall be made by a majority vote of the members present and voting.

Procedure

Article 68

The Economic and Social Council shall set up commissions in economic and social fields and for the promotion of human rights, and such other commissions as may be required for the performance of its functions.

Article 69

The Economic and Social Council shall invite any Member of the United Nations to participate, without vote, in its deliberations on any matter of particular concern to that Member.

Article 70

The Economic and Social Council may make arrangements for representatives of the specialized agencies to participate, without vote, in its deliberations and in those of the commissions established by it, and for its representatives to participate in the deliberations of the specialized agencies.

Article 71

The Economic and Social Council may make suitable arrangements for consultation with non-governmental organizations which are concerned with matters within its competence. Such arrangements may be made with international organizations and, where appropriate, with national organizations after consultation with the Member of the United Nations concerned.

Article 72

1. The Economic and Social Council shall adopt its own rules of procedure, including the method of selecting its President.

2. The Economic and Social Council shall meet as required in accordance with its rules, which shall include provision for the convening of meetings on the request of a majority of its members.

Voting

Article 71

1. Each Member of the Economic and Social Council shall have one vote.

2. Decisions of the Economic and Social Council shall be made by a majority of the Members present and voting.

Procedure

Article 72

The Economic and Social Council shall set up commissions in economic and social fields, commissions for the promotion of human rights, and such other commissions as may be required for the performance of its functions.

Article 73

The Economic and Social Council shall invite any Member of the United Nations to participate, without vote, in its deliberations on any matter of particular concern to that Member.

The Economic and Social Council may invite any Member to participate, without vote, in its deliberations.

Article 74

The Economic and Social Council may make arrangements for representatives of the specialized agencies to participate, without vote, in its deliberations and in those of the commissions established by it, and for its representatives to participate in the deliberations of the specialized agencies.

Article 75

The Economic and Social Council may make suitable arrangements for consultation with nongovernmental organizations that are concerned with matters within its competence. Such arrangements may be made with international organizations and, where appropriate, with national organizations after consultation with the Member of the United Nations concerned.

Article 76

1. The Economic and Social Council shall adopt its own rules of procedure, including the method of selecting its President.

2. The Economic and Social Council shall meet as required in accordance with its rules, which shall include provisions for the convening of meetings on the request of a majority of its Members.

Chapter XIII
THE TRUSTEESHIP COUNCIL

Composition

Article 86

1. The Trusteeship Council shall consist of the following Members of the United Nations:

a. those Members administering trust territories;

b. such of those Members mentioned by name in Article 23 as are not administering trust territories; and

c. as many other Members elected for three-year terms by the General Assembly as may be necessary to ensure that the total number of members of the Trusteeship Council is equally divided between those Members of the United Nations which administer trust territories and those which do not.

2. Each member of the Trusteeship Council shall designate one specially qualified person to represent it therein.

Functions and Powers

Article 87

The General Assembly and, under its authority, the Trusteeship Council, in carrying out their functions, may:

a. consider reports submitted by the administering authority;

b. accept petitions and examine them in consultation with the administering authority;

c. provide for periodic visits to the respective trust territories at times agreed upon with the administering authority; and

d. take these and other actions in conformity with the terms of the trusteeship agreements.

Chapter XI
THE TRUSTEESHIP COUNCIL

Composition

Article 77

1. The Trusteeship Council shall consist of the following Members of the United Nations:

a. those Members administering Trust Territories;

b. such of those Members mentioned by name in Article 23 as are not administering Trust Territories; and

c. as many other Members elected for three-year terms by the General Assembly as may be necessary to ensure that the total number of Members of the Trusteeship Council is equally divided between those Members of the United Nations that administer Trust Territories and those that do not.

2. Each Member of the Trusteeship Council shall designate one specially qualified person to represent it therein.

Functions and Powers

Article 78

The General Assembly and, under its authority, the Trusteeship Council, in carrying out their functions, may:

a. consider reports submitted by the administering authority;

b. accept petitions and examine them in consultation with the administering authority;

c. provide for periodic visits to the respective Trust Territories at times agreed upon with the administering authority; and

d. take these and other actions in conformity with the terms of the trusteeship agreements.

The Trusteeship Council may provide for periodic visits to the respective Trust Territories.

Article 88

The Trusteeship Council shall formulate a questionnaire on the political, economic, social, and educational advancement of the inhabitants of each trust territory, and the administering authority for each trust territory within the competence of the General Assembly shall make an annual report to the General Assembly upon the basis of such questionnaire.

Voting

Article 89

1. Each member of the Trusteeship Council shall have one vote.

2. Decisions of the Trusteeship Council shall be made by a majority of the members present and voting.

Procedure

Article 90

1. The Trusteeship Council shall adopt its own rules of procedure, including the method of selecting its President.

2. The Trusteeship Council shall meet as required in accordance with its rules, which shall include provision for the convening of meetings on the request of a majority of its members.

Article 91

The Trusteeship Council shall, when appropriate, avail itself of the assistance of the Economic and Social Council and of the specialized agencies in regard to matters with which they are respectively concerned.

Article 79

The Trusteeship Council shall formulate a questionnaire on the political, economic, social, and educational advancement of the inhabitants of each Trust Territory, and the administering authority for each Trust Territory within the competence of the General Assembly shall make an annual report to the General Assembly upon the basis of such questionnaire.

Voting

Article 80

1. Each Member of the Trusteeship Council shall have one vote.

2. Decisions of the Trusteeship Council shall be made by a majority of the Members present and voting.

Procedure

Article 81

1. The Trusteeship Council shall adopt its own rules of procedure, including the method of selecting its President.

2. The Trusteeship Council shall meet as required in accordance with its rules, which shall include provision for the convening of meetings on the request of a majority of its Members.

Article 82

The Trusteeship Council shall, when appropriate, avail itself of the Economic and Social Council and of the specialized agencies in regard to matters with which they are respectively concerned.

The Trusteeship Council shall formulate a questionnaire on the political, economic, social, and educational advancement of the inhabitants of each Trust Territory.

Chapter XIV
THE INTERNATIONAL COURT OF JUSTICE

Article 92

The International Court of Justice shall be the principal judicial organ of the United Nations. It shall function in accordance with the annexed Statute, which is based upon the Statute of the Permanent Court of International Justice and forms an integral part of the present Charter.

Article 93

1. All Members of the United Nations are *ipso facto* parties to the Statute of the International Court of Justice.

2. A state which is not a Member of the United Nations may become a party to the Statute of the International Court of Justice on conditions to be determined in each case by the General Assembly upon the recommendation of the Security Council.

Article 94

1. Each Member of the United Nations undertakes to comply with the decision of the International Court of Justice in any case to which it is a party.

2. If any party to a case fails to perform the obligations incumbent upon it under a judgment rendered by the Court, the other party may have recourse to the Security Council, which may, if it deems necessary, make recommendations or decide upon measures to be taken to give effect to the judgment.

Article 95

Nothing in the present Charter shall prevent Members of the United Nations from entrusting the solution of their differences to other tribunals by virtue of agreements already in existence or which may be concluded in the future.

Article 96

1. The General Assembly or the Security Council may request the International Court of Justice to give an advisory opinion on any legal question.

2. Other organs of the United Nations and specialized agencies, which may at any time be so authorized by the General Assembly, may also request advisory opinions of the Court on legal questions arising within the scope of their activities.

Chapter XII
THE INTERNATIONAL COURT OF JUSTICE

Article 83

The International Court of Justice shall be the principal judicial organ of the United Nations. It shall function in accordance with terms to be determined and annexed to this Chapter, and based upon the Statute of the Permanent Court of International Justice.

Article 84

1. All Members of the United Nations are ipso facto parties to the Statute of the International Court of Justice.

2. A state that is not a Member of the United Nations may become a party to the Statute of the International Court of Justice on conditions to be determined in each case by the General Assembly upon the recommendation of the Security Council.

Article 85

1. Each Member of the United Nations undertakes to comply with the decision of the International Court of Justice in any case to which it is a party.

2. If any party to a case fails to perform the obligations incumbent upon it under a judgment rendered by the Court, the other party may have recourse to the Security Council, which may, if it deems necessary, make recommendations or decide upon measures to be taken to give effect to the judgment.

Article 86

Nothing in the present Charter shall prevent Members of the United Nations from entrusting the solution of their differences to other tribunals by virtue of agreements already in existence or that may be concluded in the future.

Article 87

1. The General Assembly or the Security Council or the Central Cabinet of Administrators may request the International Court of Justice to give an advisory opinion on any legal question.

2. Other organs of the United Nations and specialized agencies, which may at any time be so authorized by the General Assembly, may also request advisory opinions of the Court on legal questions arising within the scope of their activities.

*E*ach Member undertakes to comply with the decision of the International Court of Justice in any case to which it is a party.

NOTE—No parallel provisions
in the original 1945
United Nations Charter

Chapter XIII
WORLD PANEL OF MEDIATORS

Article 88

The World Panel of Mediators shall consist of not fewer than three mediators nor more than fifteen mediators appointed by the Secretary-General with the advice and consent of the Central Cabinet of Administrators. Appointments may be for a fixed term, or for life, subject to mandatory retirement at age 70, and, in any event, shall be subject to impeachment and removal by a three-fourths vote of the Central Council of Administrators.

Article 89

The World Panel of Mediators shall act in international disputes through the assignment of one Member of the Panel to a specific dispute.

Article 90

The recommendations or decisions or conclusions of the World Panel of Mediators shall not in any event be binding or mandatory upon the parties to a dispute, and shall only be effective upon agreement by the parties to a dispute.

Article 91

Mediation by the World Panel of Mediators may be requested by any one or more parties to a dispute. The assignment of a mediator to a specific dispute may also be requested of the World Panel of Mediators by the Secretary-General or by any one of the principal organs of the United Nations.

Article 92

The World Panel of Mediators shall organize its work, establish its procedures, and develop its methods within the provisions of this Charter.

Mediation by the World Panel of Mediators may be requested by any one or more parties to a dispute.

NOTE—No parallel provisions
in the original 1945
United Nations Charter

Chapter XIV
WORLD BOARD OF ARBITRATION

Article 93

The World Board of Arbitration shall consist of nine Members appointed by the Secretary-General with the advice and consent of the Central Cabinet Administrators. Appointments shall be for life, subject to mandatory retirement at the age of 70, and subject to impeachment and removal by a three-fourths vote of the Central Cabinet of Administrators.

Article 94

Not more than one Member of the World Board of Arbitration may be a citizen of any one Member state.

Article 95

The World Board of Arbitration may take jurisdiction over any international dispute only if all parties to the dispute agree voluntarily to the jurisdiction, and only if all parties agree to be bound by and to accept in good faith the decision of the World Board of Arbitrators.

The World Board of Arbitration may take jurisdiction of any international dispute only if all parties to the dispute agree voluntarily to the jurisdiction.

Article 96

The World Board of Arbitrators may act with its full membership, or with any lesser number agreed upon by the parties to the dispute. If a lesser number is to act, the arbitrators participating shall be selected by lot, excluding any individual arbitrators who are citizens of one of the parties to the dispute. Alternatively, all parties may agree to the identity of the arbitrator or arbitrators for a specific dispute.

Article 97

All decisions of the World Board of Arbitrators shall be in writing, shall be signed by the arbitrators, and shall be published.

Article 98

Nothing shall prevent the parties to a dispute from reaching a voluntary agreement during the process of arbitration and prior to the decision of the World Board of Arbitration.

Article 99

The Secretary-General, and any of the other principal organs of the United Nations, may recommend the submission of a dispute to the World Board of Arbitration, but such submission may not be required or mandatory.

NOTE—No parallel provisions
in the original 1945
United Nations Charter

Chapter XV
WORLD COURT OF EQUITY

Article 100

A World Court of Equity is established with worldwide equitable jurisdiction as herein set forth.

Article 101

The World Court of Equity shall not have jurisdiction over any matter within the jurisdiction of the International Court of Justice.

Article 102

The World Court of Equity shall have jurisdiction over any dispute between two or more Member states whenever one Member state petitions the Court to take jurisdiction.

Article 103

The World Court of Equity may consider all facts and circumstances it deems relevant to a fair, just, and equitable decision in a matter before it and shall give consideration to, but not be restricted to or preempted by, treaties or other international agreements, except for the Charter of the United Nations, which shall be the basic law applied by the Court.

Article 104

Eleven justices shall be elected by the voting rights of Member states for a term of life, or until mandatory retirement at the age of 70 years.

Article 105

Justices may be impeached by a two-thirds voting rights of Member states, taken after a hearing upon written charges of malfeasance or misfeasance in office.

Article 106

Not more than one justice shall be a citizen of any one Member state.

Article 107

Three or more justices may constitute a regional equity court, or a special purpose equity court, when so established by the majority vote of the entire Court.

A World Court of Equity is established with worldwide equitable jurisdiction as herein set forth.

Chapter XV
THE SECRETARIAT

Article 97

The Secretariat shall comprise a Secretary-General and such staff as the Organization may require. The Secretary-General shall be appointed by the General Assembly upon the recommendation of the Security Council. He shall be the chief administrative officer of the Organization.

Article 98

The Secretary-General shall act in that capacity in all meetings of the General Assembly, of the Security Council, of the Economic and Social Council, and of the Trusteeship Council, and shall perform such other functions as are entrusted to him by these organs. The Secretary-General shall make an annual report to the General Assembly on the work of the Organization.

Article 99

The Secretary-General may bring to the attention of the Security Council any matter which in his opinion may threaten the maintenance of international peace and security.

Article 100

1. In the performance of their duties the Secretary-General and the staff shall not seek or receive instructions from any government or from any other authority external to the Organization. They shall refrain from any action which might reflect on their position as international officials responsible only to the Organization.

2. Each Member of the United Nations undertakes to respect the exclusively international character of the responsibilities of the Secretary-General and the staff and not to seek to influence them in the discharge of their responsibilities.

Article 108

An individual or group of individuals, with the consent of the Member state in which they are citizens, or of the Member state in which they are domiciled for at least three years, may apply to the World Court of Equity in any case on the grounds that no other judicial recourse is reasonably open to obtain equity, and in that event, the World Court of Equity, at its discretion, may take jurisdiction in such matters.

Chapter XVI
THE SECRETARIAT

Article 109

The Secretariat shall comprise a Secretary-General and such staff as the organization may require. The Secretary-General shall be appointed by the General Assembly upon the recommendation of the Security Council. He or she shall be the chief administrative officer of the Organization.

Article 110

The Secretary-General shall act in that capacity in all meetings of the General Assembly, of the Security Council, of the Economic and Social Council, and of the Trusteeship Council, and shall perform such other functions as are entrusted to him or her by these organs. The Secretary-General shall serve as Chairman of the Central Cabinet of Administrators. The Secretary-General shall make an annual report to the General Assembly on the work of the Organization.

Article 111

The Secretary-General may bring to the attention of the Security Council any matter that in his or her opinion may threaten the maintenance of international peace and security.

Article 112

1. In the performance of their duties the Secretary-General and the staff shall not seek or receive instructions from any government or from any other authority external to the Organization. They shall refrain from any action that might reflect on their positions as international officials responsible to the Organization.

2. Each Member of the United Nations undertakes to respect the exclusively international character of the responsibilities of the Secretary-General and the staff and agrees not to seek to influence them in the discharge of their responsibilities.

An individual or group of individuals may apply to the World Court of Equity when no other judicial recourse is reasonably open to obtain equity.

Article 101

1. The staff shall be appointed by the Secretary-General under regulations established by the General Assembly.

2. Appropriate staffs shall be permanently assigned to the Economic and Social Council, the Trusteeship Council, and, as required, to other organs of the United Nations. These staffs shall form a part of the Secretariat.

3. The paramount consideration in the employment of the staff and in the determination of the conditions of service shall be the necessity of securing the highest standards of efficiency, competence, and integrity. Due regard shall be paid to the importance of recruiting the staff on as wide a geographical basis as possible.

Article 113

1. The staff shall be appointed by the Secretary-General under the regulations established by the General Assembly.

2. Appropriate staffs shall be permanently assigned to the Central Cabinet of Administrators, the Economic and Social Council, the Trusteeship Council, and, as required, other organs of the United Nations. These staffs form a part of the Secretariat.

3. The permanent consideration in the employment of the staff and in the determination of the conditions of service shall be the necessity of securing the highest standards of efficiency, competence, and integrity. Due regard shall be paid to the importance of recruiting the staff on as wide a geographical basis as possible.

The staff shall be appointed by the Secretary-General under the regulations established by the General Assembly.

Chapter VI
PACIFIC SETTLEMENT OF DISPUTES

Article 33

1. The parties to any dispute, the continuance of which is likely to endanger the maintenance of international peace and security, shall, first of all, seek a solution by negotiation, enquiry, mediation, conciliation, arbitration, judicial settlement, resort to regional agencies or arrangements, or other peaceful means of their own choice.

2. The Security Council shall, when it deems necessary, call upon the parties to settle their dispute by such means.

Article 34

The Security Council may investigate any dispute, or any situation which might lead to international friction or give rise to a dispute, in order to determine whether the continuance of the dispute or situation is likely to endanger the maintenance of international peace and security.

Article 35

1. Any Member of the United Nations may bring any dispute, or any situation of the nature referred to in Article 34, to the attention of the Security Council or of the General Assembly.

2. A state which is not a Member of the United Nations may bring to the attention of the Security Council or of the General Assembly any dispute to which it is a party if it accepts in advance, for the purposes of the dispute, the obligations of pacific settlement provided in the present Charter.

3. The proceedings of the General Assembly in respect of matters brought to its attention under this Article will be subject to the provisions of Articles 11 and 12.

Chapter XVII
PACIFIC SETTLEMENT OF DISPUTES

Article 114

1. The parties to any dispute, the continuance of which is likely to endanger the maintenance of international peace and security, shall, first of all, seek a solution by negotiation, enquiry, mediation, conciliation, arbitration, judicial settlement, resort to regional agencies or arrangements, or other peaceful means of their own choice.

2. The Security Council shall, when it deems necessary, call upon the parties to settle their disputes by such means.

3. Within one year after the effective date of this Charter, and annually thereafter, each Member shall notify the Secretary-General in writing of any disputes of any nature with one or more other states that have been pending for a period of more than one year, stating in a concise summary the nature of the dispute and the status of efforts to reach a settlement.

Article 115

The Security Council may investigate any dispute, or any situation that might lead to a dispute or to international friction, in order to determine whether the continuance of the dispute or situation is likely to endanger the maintenance of international peace and security.

Article 116

1. Any Member of the United Nations may bring any dispute, or any situation of the nature referred to in Articles 114 and 115, to the attention of the Security Council or of the General Assembly.

2. A state that is not a Member of the United Nations may bring to the attention of the Security Council or of the General Assembly any dispute to which it is a party if it accepts in advance, for the purposes of the dispute, the obligations of pacific settlement provided in this Charter.

3. The proceedings of the General Assembly in respect to matters brought to its attention under this Article will be subject to the provisions of Article 24.

The parties to any dispute shall, first of all, seek a solution by negotiation, enquiry, mediation, conciliation, arbitration, judicial settlement, or other peaceful means.

Article 36

1. The Security Council may, at any stage of a dispute of the nature referred to in Article 33 or of a situation of like nature, recommend appropriate procedures or methods of adjustment.

2. The Security Council should take into consideration any procedures for the settlement of the dispute which have already been adopted by the parties.

3. In making recommendations under this Article the Security Council should also take into consideration that legal disputes should as a general rule be referred by the parties to the International Court of Justice in accordance with the provisions of the Statute of the Court.

Article 37

1. Should the parties to a dispute of the nature referred to in Article 33 fail to settle it by the means indicated in that Article, they shall refer it to the Security Council.

2. If the Security Council deems that the continuance of the dispute is in fact likely to endanger the maintenance of international peace and security, it shall decide whether to take action under Article 36 or to recommend such terms of settlement as it may consider appropriate.

Article 38

Without prejudice to the provisions of Articles 33 to 37, the Security Council may, if all the parties to any dispute so request, make recommendations to the parties with a view to a pacific settlement of the dispute.

Article 117

1. The Security Council may, at any stage of a dispute of the nature referred to in Articles 114 and 115 or of a situation of like nature, recommend appropriate procedures or methods of adjustment.

2. The Security Council should take into consideration any procedures for the settlement of the dispute that have already been adopted by the parties.

3. In making recommendations under this Article, the Security Council should also take into consideration that legal disputes should as a general rule be referred by the parties to the International Court of Justice in accordance with the provisions of the Statute of the Court.

Article 118

1. Should the parties to a dispute of the nature referred to in Articles 114 and 115 fail to settle it by the means indicated, they shall refer it to the Security Council.

2. If the Security Council deems that the continuance of the dispute is in fact likely to endanger the maintenance of international peace and security, it shall decide whether to take action under Chapter XVIII or whether to recommend such terms of settlement as it may consider appropriate.

The Security Council should take into consideration any procedures for the settlement of the dispute that have already been adopted by the parties.

Chapter VII
ACTION WITH RESPECT TO THREATS TO THE PEACE, BREACHES OF THE PEACE, AND ACTS OF AGGRESSION

Article 39

The Security Council shall determine the existence of any threat to the peace, breach of the peace, or act of aggression and shall make recommendations, or decide what measures shall be taken in accordance with Articles 41 and 42, to maintain or restore international peace and security.

Article 40

In order to prevent an aggravation of the situation, the Security Council may, before making the recommendations or deciding upon the measures provided for in Article 39, call upon the parties concerned to comply with such provisional measures as it deems necessary or desirable. Such provisional measures shall be without prejudice to the rights, claims, or position of the parties concerned. The Security Council shall duly take account of failure to comply with such provisional measures.

Article 41

The Security Council may decide what measures not involving the use of armed force are to be employed to give effect to its decisions, and it may call upon the Members of the United Nations to apply such measures. These may include complete or partial interruption of economic relations and of rail, sea, air, postal, telegraphic, radio, and other means of communications, and the severance of diplomatic relations.

Article 42

Should the Security Council consider that measures provided for in Article 41 would be inadequate or have proved to be inadequate, it may take such action by air, sea, or land forces as may be necessary to maintain or restore international peace and security. Such action may include demonstrations, blockade, and other operations by air, sea, or land forces of Members of the United Nations.

Chapter XVIII
ACTION WITH RESPECT TO THREATS TO THE PEACE, BREACHES OF THE PEACE, AND ACTS OF AGGRESSION

Article 119

The Security Council shall determine the existence of any threat to the peace, breach of the peace, or act of aggression, and shall make recommendations, or decide what measure shall be taken, in accordance with Articles 120, 121, and 122 to maintain or restore international peace and security.

Article 120

In order to prevent an aggravation of the situation, the Security Council may, before making the recommendations or deciding upon the measures provided for in Articles 121, 122, and 123, call upon the parties concerned to comply with a cease-fire or such other provisional measures as it deems necessary or desirable. Such provisional measures shall be without prejudice to the rights, claims, or position of the parties concerned. The Security Council shall duly take account of failure to comply with such provisional measures.

Article 121

The Security Council may decide what measures not involving the use of armed force are to be employed to give effect to its decisions, and it may call upon the Members of the United Nations to apply such measures. These may include complete or partial interruption of economic relations; complete or partial interruption of rail, sea, air, postal, radio, telegraphic, and other means of communication; and the severance of diplomatic relations.

Article 122

Should the Security Council consider that measures provided for in Articles 120 and 121 would be inadequate or have proved to be inadequate, it may take such action by the United Nations Peace Force, or by other air, sea, or land forces, or both, as may be necessary to maintain or restore international peace and security. Such action may include demonstrations, blockade, and other operations by air, sea, or land forces of Members of the United Nations.

The Security Council shall determine the existence of any threat to the peace.

Article 43

1. All Members of the United Nations, in order to contribute to the maintenance of international peace and security, undertake to make available to the Security Council, on its call and in accordance with a special agreement or agreements, armed forces, assistance, and facilities, including rights of passage, necessary for the purpose of maintaining international peace and security.

2. Such agreement or agreements shall govern the numbers and types of forces, their degree of readiness and general location, and the nature of the facilities and assistance to be provided.

3. The agreement or agreements shall be negotiated as soon as possible on the initiative of the Security Council. They shall be concluded between the Security Council and Members or between the Security Council and groups of Members and shall be subject to ratification by the signatory states in accordance with their respective constitutional processes.

Article 44

When the Security Council has decided to use force it shall, before calling upon a Member not represented on it to provide armed forces in fulfilment of the obligations assumed under Article 43, invite that Member, if the Member so desires, to participate in the decisions of the Security Council concerning the employment of contingents of that Member's armed forces.

Article 45

In order to enable the United Nations to take urgent military measures, Members shall hold immediately available national air-force contingents for combined international enforcement action. The strength and degree of readiness of these contingents and plans for their combined action shall be determined, within the limits laid down in the special agreement or agreements referred to in Article 43, by the Security Council with the assistance of the Military Staff Committee.

Article 46

Plans for the application of armed force shall be made by the Security Council with the assistance of the Military Staff Committee.

Article 47

1. There shall be established a Military Staff Committee to advise and assist the Security Council on all questions relating to the Security Council's military requirements for the maintenance of international peace and security, the employment and command of forces placed at its disposal, the regulation of armaments, and possible disarmament.

Article 123

1. All Members of the United Nations, in order to contribute to the maintenance of international peace and security, shall undertake to make available to the Security Council, on its call and in accordance with a special agreement or agreements, armed forces, assistance, and facilities, including rights of passage, necessary for the purpose of maintaining international peace and security.

2. Such agreement or agreements shall govern the number and types of forces, their degree of readiness and general location, and the nature of the facilities and assistance to be provided.

3. The agreement or agreements shall be negotiated as soon as possible on the initiative of the Security Council. They shall be concluded between the Security Council and Members or between the Security Council and groups of Members and shall be subject to ratification of the signatory states in accordance with their respective constitutional processes.

Article 124

When the Security Council has decided to use force, it shall, before calling upon a Member not represented on it to provide armed forces in fulfillment of the obligations under this Charter, invite that Member, if the Member so desires, to participate in the decisions of the Security Council concerning the employment of contingents of that Member's armed forces.

Article 125

In order to enable the United Nations to take urgent military measures, Members shall hold immediately available national air force contingents for combined international enforcement action. The strength and degree of readiness of these contingents and plans for their combined action shall be determined within the limits laid down in special agreements with the Security Council.

Article 126

Plans for the application of armed force shall be made by the Security Council.

All Members of the United Nations, in order to contribute to the maintenance of international peace and security, shall undertake to make available to the Security Council armed forces, assistance, and facilities necessary for maintaining international peace and security.

2. The Military Staff Committee shall consist of the Chiefs of Staff of the permanent members of the Security Council or their representatives. Any Member of the United Nations not permanently represented on the Committee shall be invited by the Committee to be associated with it when the efficient discharge of the Committee's responsibilities requires the participation of that Member in its work.

3. The Military Staff Committee shall be responsible under the Security Council for the strategic direction of any armed forces placed at the disposal of the Security Council. Questions relating to the command of such forces shall be worked out subsequently.

4. The Military Staff Committee, with the authorization of the Security Council and after consultation with appropriate regional agencies, may establish regional sub-committees.

Article 48

1. The action required to carry out the decisions of the Security Council for the maintenance of international peace and security shall be taken by all the Members of the United Nations or by some of them, as the Security Council may determine.

2. Such decisions shall be carried out by the Members of the United Nations directly and through their action in the appropriate international agencies of which they are members.

Article 49

The Members of the United Nations shall join in affording mutual assistance in carrying out the measures decided upon by the Security Council.

Article 50

If preventive or enforcement measures against any state are taken by the Security Council, any other state, whether a Member of the United Nations or not, which finds itself confronted with special economic problems arising from the carrying out of those measures shall have the right to consult the Security Council with regard to a solution of those problems.

Article 51

Nothing in the present Charter shall impair the inherent right of individual or collective self-defence if an armed attack occurs against a Member of the United Nations, until the Security Council has taken measures necessary to maintain international peace and security. Measures taken by Members in the exercise of this right of self-defence shall be immediately reported to the Security Council and shall not in any way affect the authority and responsibility of the Security Council under the present Charter to take at any time such action as it deems necessary in order to maintain or restore international peace and security.

Article 127

1. The action required to carry out the decisions of the Security Council for the maintenance of international peace and security shall be taken by all Members of the United Nations, or by some of them, as the Security Council may determine.

2. Such decisions shall be carried out by the Members of the United Nations directly and through their action in the appropriate international agencies of which they are Members.

Article 128

The Members of the United Nations shall join in affording mutual assistance in carrying out the measures decided upon by the Security Council.

Article 129

If preventive or enforcement measures against any state are taken by the Security Council, any other state—whether a Member of the United Nations or not—that finds itself confronted with special economic problems arising from the carrying out of those measures shall have the right to consult the Security Council with regard to a solution of those problems.

Article 130

Nothing in the present Charter shall impair the inherent right of individual or collective self-defense if an armed attack occurs against a Member of the United Nations, until the Security Council has taken the measures necessary to maintain international peace and security. Measures taken by Members in the exercise of this right of self-defense shall be immediately reported to the Security Council and shall not in any way affect the authority and responsibility of the Security Council under this Charter to take at any time such action as it deems necessary in order to maintain or restore international peace or security.

The Members shall join in affording mutual assistance in carrying out the measures decided upon by the Security Council.

Chapter IX
INTERNATIONAL ECONOMIC AND SOCIAL CO-OPERATION

Article 55

With a view to the creation of conditions of stability and well-being which are necessary for peaceful and friendly relations among nations based on respect for the principle of equal rights and self-determination of peoples, the United Nations shall promote:

a. higher standards of living, full employment, and conditions of economic and social progress and development;

b. solutions of international economic, social, health, and related problems; and international cultural and educational cooperation; and

c. universal respect for, and observance of, human rights and fundamental freedoms for all without distinction as to race, sex, language, or religion.

Article 56

All Members pledge themselves to take joint and separate action in cooperation with the Organization for the achievement of the purposes set forth in Article 55.

Article 57

1. The various specialized agencies, established by intergovernmental agreement and defined in their basic instruments, in economic, social, cultural, educational, health, and related fields, shall be brought into relationship with the United Nations in accordance with the provisions of Article 63.

2. Such agencies thus brought into relationship with the United Nations are hereinafter referred to as specialized agencies.

Chapter XIX
INTERNATIONAL ECONOMIC AND SOCIAL CO-OPERATION

Article 131

With a view to the creation of conditions of stability and well-being that are necessary for peaceful and friendly relations among nations based on respect for the principle of equal rights and self-determination of peoples, the United Nations shall promote:

(a) higher standards of living, full employment, and conditions of economic and social progress and development;

(b) solutions of international economic, social, health, and related problems; and international cultural and educational cooperation;

(c) universal respect for, and observance of, human rights and fundamental freedoms for all, without discrimination as to race, sex, language, or religion;

(d) improvement and safeguarding of the environment of the earth and of the universe against pollution of air, water, and land; and

(e) humanitarian and expert aid in earthquakes, hurricanes, typhoons, volcanic eruptions, nuclear accidents, and other major disasters.

The United Nations shall promote higher standards of living, full employment, and conditions of economic and social progress.

Article 132

All Members pledge themselves to take joint and separate action in cooperation with the Organization for the achievement of the purposes set forth in Article 131.

Article 133

1. The various specialized agencies, established by intergovernmental agreement and having wide international responsibilities, as defined in their basic instruments, in economic, social, cultural, educational, health, and related fields, shall be brought into relationship with the United Nations in accordance with the provisions of Article 68.

2. Such agencies thus brought into relationship with the United Nations are herein referred to as specialized agencies.

Article 58

The Organization shall make recommendations for the co-ordination of the policies and activities of the specialized agencies.

Article 59

The Organization shall, where appropriate, initiate negotiations among the states concerned for the creation of any new specialized agencies required for the accomplishment of the purposes set forth in Article 55.

Article 60

Responsibility for the discharge of the functions of the Organization set forth in this Chapter shall be vested in the General Assembly and, under the authority of the General Assembly, in the Economic and Social Council, which shall have for this purpose the powers set forth in Chapter X.

Article 134

The Organization shall make recommendations for the coordination of the policies and activities of the specialized agencies.

Article 135

The Organization shall, where appropriate, initiate negotiations among the states concerned for the creation of any new specialized agencies required for the accomplishment of the purposes set forth in Article 131.

Article 136

Responsibility for the discharge of the functions of the Organization set forth in this Chapter shall be vested in the General Assembly, and, under the authority of the General Assembly, in the Economic and Social Council, which shall have for this purpose the powers set forth in Chapter X.

The United Nations shall promote humanitarian and expert aid in earthquakes, hurricanes, typhoons, volcanic eruptions, nuclear accidents, and other major disasters.

Chapter XI
DECLARATION REGARDING NON-SELF-GOVERNING TERRITORIES

Article 73

Members of the United Nations which have or assume responsibilities for the administration of territories whose peoples have not yet attained a full measure of self-government recognize the principle that the interests of the inhabitants of these territories are paramount, and accept as a sacred trust the obligation to promote to the utmost, within the system of international peace and security established by the present Charter, the well-being of the inhabitants of these territories, and, to this end:

a. to ensure, with due respect for the culture of the peoples concerned, their political, economic, social, and educational advancement, their just treatment, and their protection against abuses;

b. to develop self-government, to take due account of the political aspirations of the peoples, and to assist them in the progressive development of their free political institutions, according to the particular circumstances of each territory and its peoples and their varying stages of advancement;

c. to further international peace and security;

d. to promote constructive measures of development, to encourage research, and to co-operate with one another and, when and where appropriate, with specialized international bodies with a view to the practical achievement of the social, economic, and scientific purposes set forth in this Article; and

e. to transmit regularly to the Secretary-General for information purposes, subject to such limitation as security and constitutional considerations may require, statistical and other information of a technical nature relating to economic, social, and educational conditions in the territories for which they are respectively responsible other than those territories to which Chapters XII and XIII apply.

Article 74

Members of the United Nations also agree that their policy in respect of the territories to which this Chapter applies, no less than in respect of their metropolitan areas, must be based on the general principle of good-neighbourliness, due account being taken of the interests and well-being of the rest of the world, in social, economic and commercial matters.

Chapter XX
DECLARATION REGARDING NON-SELF-GOVERNING TERRITORIES

Article 137

Members of the United Nations that have or assume responsibilities for the administration of territories whose peoples have not yet attained a full measure of self-government, or in territories in which the Security Council makes a finding that no effective and adequate government exists, recognize the principle that the interests of the inhabitants of these territories are paramount, and accept as a sacred trust the obligation to promote to the utmost, within the system of international peace, the well-being of the inhabitants of these territories, and, to this end:

(a) to ensure, with due respect for the culture of the peoples concerned, their political, economic, social, and educational advancement; their just treatment; and their protection against abuse;

(b) to develop self-government, to take due account of the political aspirations of the peoples, and to assist them in the progressive development of their free political institutions, according to the particular circumstances of each territory and its peoples and their varying stages of advancement;

(c) to further international peace and security;

(d) to promote constructive measures of development, to encourage research, and to cooperate with one another and, when and where appropriate, with specialized international bodies, with a view to the practical achievement of the social, economic, and scientific purpose set forth in this Article; and

(e) to transmit regularly to the Secretary-General for information purposes, subject to such limitations as security and constitutional considerations may require, statistical and other information of a technical nature relating to economic, social, and educational conditions in the territories for which they are respectively responsible, other than those territories to which Chapters XIV and XV apply.

*M*embers responsible for the administration of territories whose peoples have not yet attained self-government recognize that the interests of the inhabitants of these territories are paramount.

Article 138

Members of the United Nations also agree that their policy in respect to the territories to which this Chapter applies, no less than in respect to their metropolitan areas, must be based on the general principle of good-neighborliness, due account being taken of the interests and well-being of the rest of the world, in social, economic, and commercial matters.

Chapter XII
INTERNATIONAL TRUSTEESHIP

Article 75

The United Nations shall establish under its authority an international trusteeship system for the administration and supervision of such territories as may be placed thereunder by subsequent individual agreements. These territories are hereinafter referred to as trust territories.

Article 76

The basic objectives of the trusteeship system, in accordance with the Purposes of the United Nations laid down in Article 1 of the present Charter, shall be:

a. to further international peace and security;

b. to promote the political, economic, social, and educational advancement of the inhabitants of the trust territories, and their progressive development towards self-government or independence as may be appropriate to the particular circumstances of each territory and its peoples and the freely expressed wishes of the peoples concerned, and as may be provided by the terms of each trusteeship agreement;

c. to encourage respect for human rights and for fundamental freedoms for all without distinction as to race, sex, language, or religion, and to encourage recognition of the interdependence of the peoples of the world; and

d. to ensure equal treatment in social, economic, and commercial matters for all Members of the United Nations and their nationals, and also equal treatment for the latter in the administration of justice, without prejudice to the attainment of the foregoing objectives and subject to the provisions of Article 80.

Chapter XXI
INTERNATIONAL TRUSTEESHIP

Article 139

The United Nations shall establish under its authority an international Trusteeship System for the administration and supervision of such territories as may be placed thereunder by subsequent individual agreements or by decision of the Security Council. These territories are hereinafter referred to as Trust Territories.

Article 140

The basic objectives of the Trusteeship System, in accordance with the purposes of the United Nations laid down in Article 1 of this Charter, shall be:

(a) to further international peace and security;

(b) to promote the political, economic, social, and educational advancement of the inhabitants of the Trust Territories; and to promote their progress toward self-government or independence, as may be appropriate to the particular circumstances of each territory and its peoples and their freely expressed wishes, and as may be provided by the terms of each trusteeship agreement;

(c) to encourage respect for human rights and for fundamental freedoms for all without distinction as to race, sex, language, or religion, and to encourage recognition of the interdependence of the peoples of the world; and

(d) to ensure equal treatment in social, economic, and commercial matters for all Members of the United Nations and their nationals, and also equal treatment for the latter in the administration of justice, without prejudice to the attainment of the foregoing objectives and subject to the provisions of Article 144.

The Trusteeship System shall promote the political, economic, social, and educational advancement of the inhabitants of the Trust Territories.

Article 77

1. The trusteeship system shall apply to such territories in the following categories as may be placed thereunder by means of trusteeship agreements:

a. territories now held under mandate;

b. territories which may be detached from enemy states as a result of the Second World War; and

c. territories voluntarily placed under the system by states responsible for their administration.

2. It will be a matter for subsequent agreement as to which territories in the foregoing categories will be brought under the trusteeship system and upon what terms.

Article 78

The trusteeship system shall not apply to territories which have become Members of the United Nations, relationships among which shall be based on respect for the principle of sovereign equality.

Article 79

The terms of trusteeship for each territory to be placed under the trusteeship system, including any alteration or amendment, shall be agreed upon by the states directly concerned, including the mandatory power in the case of territories held under mandate by a Member of the United Nations, and shall be approved as provided for in Articles 83 and 85.

Article 80

1. Except as may be agreed upon in individual trusteeship agreements, made under Articles 77, 79, and 81, placing each territory under the trusteeship system, and until such agreements have been concluded, nothing in this Chapter shall be construed in or of itself to alter in any manner the rights whatsoever of any states or any peoples or the terms of existing international instruments to which Members of the United Nations may respectively be parties.

2. Paragraph 1 of this Article shall not be interpreted as giving grounds for delay or postponement of the negotiation and conclusion of agreements for placing mandated and other territories under the trusteeship system as provided for in Article 77.

Article 141

1. The Trusteeship System shall apply to such territories as may have been or may hereafter be placed thereunder by means of trusteeship agreements, or by a decision of the Security Council.

2. It will be a matter for agreement as to which territories will be brought under the Trusteeship System and on what terms.

Article 142

The Trusteeship System shall not apply to territories that have become Members of the United Nations, relationships among which shall be based on respect for the principle of sovereign equality.

Article 143

The terms of trusteeship, including alterations or amendments, for each territory to be placed under the Trusteeship System shall be agreed upon by the states directly concerned and shall be approved as provided for in Articles 147 and 149.

Article 144

1. Except as may be agreed upon in individual trusteeship agreements made under Articles 141, 143, and 145, placing each territory under the Trusteeship System, and until such agreements have been concluded, nothing in this Chapter shall be construed in or of itself to alter in any manner the rights whatsoever of any states or any peoples or the terms of existing international instruments to which Members of the United Nations may respectively be parties.

2. Paragraph 1 of this Article shall not be interpreted as giving grounds for delay or postponement of the negotiation and conclusion of agreements for placing territories under the Trusteeship System as provided for in Article 137.

The terms of trusteeship for each territory shall be agreed upon by the states directly concerned.

Article 81

The trusteeship agreement shall in each case include the terms under which the trust territory will be administered and designate the authority which will exercise the administration of the trust territory. Such authority, hereinafter called the administering authority, may be one or more states or the Organization itself.

Article 82

There may be designated, in any trusteeship agreement, a strategic area or areas which may include part or all of the trust territory to which the agreement applies, without prejudice to any special agreement or agreements made under Article 43.

Article 83

1. All functions of the United Nations relating to strategic areas, including the approval of the terms of the trusteeship agreements and of their alteration or amendment, shall be exercised by the Security Council.

2. The basic objectives set forth in Article 76 shall be applicable to the people of each strategic area.

3. The Security Council shall, subject to the provisions of the trusteeship agreements and without prejudice to security considerations, avail itself of the assistance of the Trusteeship Council to perform those functions of the United Nations under the trusteeship system relating to political, economic, social, and educational matters in the strategic areas.

Article 145

The trusteeship agreement shall in each case include the terms under which the Trust Territory will be administered and designate the authority which will exercise the administration of the Trust Territory. Such authority, hereinafter called the administering authority, may be one or more states or the Organization itself.

Article 146

There may be designated, in any trusteeship agreement, a strategic area or areas that may include part or all of the Trust Territory to which the agreement applies.

Article 147

1. All functions of the United Nations relating to strategic areas, including the approval of the terms of the trusteeship agreements and of their alteration or amendment, shall be exercised by the Security Council.

2. The basic objectives set forth in Article 137 shall be applicable to the people of each strategic area.

3. The Security Council shall, subject to the provisions of the trusteeship agreements and without prejudice to security considerations, avail itself of the assistance of the Trusteeship Council to perform those functions of the United Nations under the Trusteeship System relating to political, economic, social, and educational matters in the strategic areas.

There may be designated, in any trusteeship agreement, a strategic area or areas.

Article 84

It shall be the duty of the administering authority to ensure that the trust territory shall play its part in the maintenance of international peace and security. To this end the administering authority may make use of volunteer forces, facilities, and assistance from the trust territory in carrying out the obligations towards the Security Council undertaken in this regard by the administering authority, as well as for local defence and the maintenance of law and order within the trust territory.

Article 85

1. The functions of the United Nations with regard to trusteeship agreements for all areas not designated as strategic, including the approval of the terms of the trusteeship agreements and of their alteration or amendment, shall be exercised by the General Assembly.

2. The Trusteeship Council, operating under the authority of the General Assembly, shall assist the General Assembly in carrying out these functions.

Article 148

It shall be the duty of the administering authority to ensure that the Trust Territory shall play its part in the maintenance of international peace and security. To this end, the administering authority may make use of volunteer forces, facilities, and assistance from the Trust Territory in carrying out the obligations toward the Security Council undertaken in this regard by the administering authority, as well as for local defense and the maintenance of law and order within the Trust Territory.

Article 149

1. The function of the United Nations with regard to trusteeship agreements for all areas not designated as strategic, including the approval of the terms of the trusteeship agreement and of their alteration or amendment, shall be exercised by the General Assembly.

2. The Trusteeship Council, operating under the authority of the General Assembly, shall assist the General Assembly in carrying out these functions.

The function of the United Nations with regard to trusteeship agreements for all areas not designated as strategic, including the approval of the terms of the trusteeship agreement and of their alteration or amendment, shall be exercised by the General Assembly.

NOTE—No parallel provisions
in the original 1945
United Nations Charter

Chapter XXII
OUTER SPACE AND SEA BEDS

Article 150

The United Nations is hereby granted and declared to have sovereign jurisdiction over those elements of the universe that are not now within the sovereign jurisdiction of any Member or non-Member state, including specifically the bed of the seas beyond the jurisdiction of the Member and non-Member states, and the outer space of the universe beyond the jurisdiction of Member and non-Member states.

Article 151

The administration of the sovereign jurisdiction of elements as set forth in Article 150 shall be under the authority of the Central Cabinet of Administrators.

The United Nations is hereby granted and declared to have sovereign jurisdiction over those elements of the universe not now within the sovereign jurisdiction of any state.

NOTE—No parallel provisions
in the original 1945
United Nations Charter

Chapter XXIII
FINANCIAL SUPPORT

Article 152

A one-half of one percent duty shall be paid to the United Nations upon all international movement between Member states of all tangible goods, materials, machineries, and tangible objects of every type and designation for purposes of sale, or for purposes of lease substantially equivalent to sale. Such one-half of one percent shall be upon the valuation for purposes of sale, or upon the fair market price if the valuation for purposes of sale cannot be ascertained. One-fourth of one percent shall be paid by the exporting Member state, and one-fourth of one percent shall be paid by the importing Member state. This United Nations duty shall be reported and paid monthly by all Member states.

Article 153

The annual budget of the United Nations shall be approved by the Central Cabinet of Administrators.

Article 154

The financial accounts of the United Nations shall be audited by the Central Cabinet of Administrators.

Article 155

All Members shall receive an audited annual account of the finances of the United Nations Organization not later than five months after the end of the financial year.

Article 156

If additional funds are necessary for the expenses of the United Nations Organization, such additional funds shall be apportioned by the General Assembly, upon consideration of a recommendation by the Central Cabinet of Administrators.

All Members shall receive an audited annual account of the finances of the United Nations Organization.

NOTE—No parallel provisions
in the original 1945
United Nations Charter

Chapter XXIV
WORLDWIDE CONFERENCE OF RELIGIONS

Article 157

On one occasion in each calendar year, during a period of time in which the General Assembly of the United Nations is not meeting, the Secretary-General shall invite the Members to send participants to take part in a two-week Worldwide Conference of Religions, and shall convene and moderate, or appoint a moderator or moderators, for the session.

Article 158

Each participant shall be required to present a statement in writing that he or she has been duly designated or appointed or elected by a generally recognized religious organization within the geographic area of the United Nations Member.

Article 159

Each participant shall also be required to present, as a precondition of attending, a signed statement of the following first sentences of the Preamble to this Charter: *We the peoples of the world determined to save our own and succeeding generations from the scourge of world war, which in this age of nuclear bombs and other weapons of mass destruction carries a catastrophic threat to all humanity; and further determined to establish circumstances within which peoples of different races, varied religions, divergent ethnic origins, and a range of economic circumstances may live together in neighbor states and within individual states, without violence, and with mutual rights, justice, and progress.*

Article 160

The Worldwide Conference of Religions shall not be authorized to pass any resolutions or take any actions binding or controlling in any manner whatsoever upon any of the religions participating or upon any of the Members of the United Nations.

Article 161

The Worldwide Conference of Religions is established exclusively in recognition that future interrelationships in the world and within member states of people of different religious faiths and beliefs will be one important factor affecting the prospects of peace or war, progress or catastrophe, and influencing the degree to which the objective of the United Nations will be fulfilled.

Determined to establish circumstances within which peoples of different religions may live together without violence, and with mutual rights, justice, and progress.

NOTE—No parallel provisions
in the original 1945
United Nations Charter

Article 162

The Worldwide Conference of Religions is established further with the recognition that personal associations and discussions in a respectful and nonthreatening environment usually have a mutually constructive and creative result.

Article 163

Each Member state shall be entitled to send one participant from each generally recognized religion within its geographic area; one additional participant for each additional one million to ten million members of the religion; one additional participant for each additional ten million to one hundred million members; and one additional participant for each additional one hundred million members.

Article 164

The Secretary-General shall establish the initial rules of procedure for the Conference. The Conference may by a two-thirds affirmative vote of participants modify and amend the rules of procedure.

Article 165

The individual participation accrediting shall be for one year only. The individual participation accrediting may be renewed, but is not to exceed five years.

Article 166

The United Nations shall provide the Assembly Hall, the interpretive services, and the security services for the Worldwide Conference of Religions, but shall not provide any other expenses or services of any type or kind to the Conference or to its participants or to its members in relation to the Conference.

The Worldwide Conference of Religions is established with the recognition that personal association in a nonthreatening environment usually has a mutually constructive and creative result.

NOTE—No parallel provisions
in the original 1945
United Nations Charter

Chapter XXV
RESEARCH INSTITUTE OF PEOPLE AND GOVERNANCE

Article 167

A Research Institute of People and Governance shall be established.

Article 168

The Research Institute shall be under the direction and supervision of a Directorate.

Article 169

Each member of the United Nations shall be entitled to appoint one Director to the Research Directorate.

Article 170

The term of the Director shall be for one five-year period, and the appointee shall not be eligible for reappointment.

Article 171

The appointee shall be required to have a minimum of three years' experience in a policy-forming position of a government and a minimum of three years' experience on the faculty of a recognized or accredited institution of learning on a college level.

Article 172

The Research Institute may issue reports upon any factor or experience of governmental structure in relation to the rights of people and the effectiveness and efficiency of government in any or all objectives of government and of peoples.

Article 173

The Research Institute shall have no authority to control or bind or commit the United Nations Organization or any Member state.

A *Research Institute of People and Governance shall be established.*

Chapter XVI
MISCELLANEOUS PROVISIONS

Article 102

1. Every treaty and every international agreement entered into by any Member of the United Nations after the present Charter comes into force shall as soon as possible be registered with the Secretariat and published by it.

2. No party to any such treaty or international agreement which has not been registered in accordance with the provisions of paragraph 1 of this Article may invoke that treaty or agreement before any organ of the United Nations.

Article 103

In the event of a conflict between the obligations of the Members of the United Nations under the present Charter and their obligations under any other international agreement, their obligations under the present Charter shall prevail.

Article 104

The Organization shall enjoy in the territory of each of its Members such legal capacity as may be necessary for the exercise of its functions and the fulfillment of its purposes.

Article 105

1. The Organization shall enjoy in the territory of each of its Members such privileges and immunities as are necessary for the fulfillment of its purposes.

2. Representatives of the Members of the United Nations and officials of the Organization shall similarly enjoy such privileges and immunities as are necessary for the independent exercise of their functions in connexion with the Organization.

3. The General Assembly may make recommendations with a view to determining the details of the application of paragraphs 1 and 2 of this Article or may propose conventions to the Members of the United Nations for this purpose.

Chapter XXVI
MISCELLANEOUS PROVISIONS

Article 174

1. Every treaty and every international agreement entered into by any Member of the United Nations after this Charter comes into force shall as soon as possible be registered with the Secretariat and published by it.

2. No party to any such treaty or international agreement that has not been registered in accordance with the provisions of Paragraph 1 of this Article may invoke that treaty or agreement before any organ of the United Nations.

Article 175

In the event of a conflict between the obligations of the Members of the United Nations under this Charter and their obligations under any other international agreement, their obligations under this Charter shall prevail.

Article 176

The Organization shall enjoy in the territory of each of its Members such legal capacity as may be necessary for the exercise of its functions and the fulfillment of its purpose.

Article 177

1. The Organization shall enjoy in the territory of each of its Members such privileges and immunities as are necessary for the fulfillment of its purposes.

2. Representatives of the Members of the United Nations and officials of the Organization shall similarly enjoy such privileges and immunities as are necessary for the independent exercise of their functions in connection with the Organization.

3. The General Assembly may make recommendations with a view to determining the details of the application of Paragraphs 1 and 2 of this Article or may propose conventions to the Members of the United Nations for this purpose.

In the event of a conflict between the obligations of this Charter and obligations under any other international agreement, obligations under this Charter shall prevail.

Chapter VIII
REGIONAL ARRANGEMENTS

Article 52

1. Nothing in the present Charter precludes the existence of regional arrangements or agencies for dealing with such matters relating to the maintenance of international peace and security as are appropriate for regional action, provided that such arrangements or agencies and their activities are consistent with the Purposes and Principles of the United Nations.

2. The Members of the United Nations entering into such arrangements or constituting such agencies shall make every effort to achieve pacific settlement of local disputes through such regional arrangements or by such regional agencies before referring them to the Security Council.

3. The Security Council shall encourage the development of pacific settlement of local disputes through such regional arrangements or by such regional agencies either on the initiative of the states concerned or by reference from the Security Council.

4. This Article in no way impairs the application of Articles 34 and 35.

Article 53

1. The Security Council shall, where appropriate, utilize such regional arrangements or agencies for enforcement action under its authority. But no enforcement action shall be taken under regional arrangements or by regional agencies without the authorization of the Security Council, with the exception of measures against any enemy state, as defined in paragraph 2 of this Article, provided for pursuant to Article 107 or in regional arrangements directed against renewal of aggressive policy on the part of any such state, until such time as the Organization may, on request of the Governments concerned, be charged with the responsibility for preventing further aggression by such a state.

2. The term enemy state as used in paragraph 1 of this Article applies to any state which during the Second World War has been an enemy of any signatory of the present Charter.

Article 54

The Security Council shall at all times be kept fully informed of activities undertaken or in contemplation under regional arrangements or by regional agencies for the maintenance of international peace and security.

Chapter XXVII
REGIONAL ARRANGEMENTS

Article 178

1. Nothing in this Charter precludes the existence of regional arrangements or agencies for dealing with such matters relating to the maintenance of international peace and security as are appropriate for regional action, provided that such arrangements or agencies and their activities are consistent with the purposes and principles of the United Nations.

2. The Members of the United Nations entering into such arrangements or constituting such agencies shall make every effort to achieve pacific settlement of local disputes through such regional arrangements or by such regional agencies before referring them to the Security Council.

3. The Security Council shall encourage the development of pacific settlement of local disputes through such regional arrangements or by such regional agencies before referring them to the Security Council.

Article 179

1. The Security Council shall, where appropriate, utilize such regional arrangements or agencies for enforcement of action under its authority. But no enforcement action shall be taken under regional arrangements or by regional agencies without the authorization of the Security Council.

Article 180

The Security Council shall at all times be kept fully informed of activities undertaken or in contemplation under regional arrangements or by regional agencies for the maintenance of international peace and security.

The Members shall make every effort to achieve pacific settlement of local disputes.

Chapter XVII
TRANSITIONAL SECURITY ARRANGEMENTS

Article 106

Pending the coming into force of such special agreements referred to in Article 43 as in the opinion of the Security Council enable it to begin the exercise of its responsibilities under Article 42, the parties to the Four-Nation Declaration, signed at Moscow, 30 October 1943, and France, shall, in accordance with the provisions of paragraph 5 of that Declaration, consult with one another and as occasion requires with other Members of the United Nations with a view to such joint action on behalf of the Organization as may be necessary for the purpose of maintaining international peace and security.

Article 107

Nothing in the present Charter shall invalidate or preclude action, in relation to any state which during the Second World War has been an enemy of any signatory to the present Charter, taken or authorized as a result of that war by the Governments having responsibility for such action.

Chapter XXVIII
TRANSITIONAL ARRANGEMENTS

Article 181

Until such time that this Charter has been ratified in accordance with Article 184, by the required minimum number of states, and until such time thereafter that the United Nations General Assembly, Security Council, and Central Cabinet of Administrators constituted by this Charter shall be appointed, the preceding United Nations Charter and all of the organs established thereunder shall in all respects be and continue in full force and effect.

Until such time that this Charter has been ratified in accordance with Article 184, the preceding United Nations Charter shall continue in full force.

Chapter XVIII
AMENDMENTS

Article 108

Amendments to the present Charter shall come into force for all Members of the United Nations when they have been adopted by a vote of two thirds of the members of the General Assembly and ratified in accordance with their respective constitutional processes by two thirds of the Members of the United Nations, including all the permanent members of the Security Council.

Article 109

1. A General Conference of the Members of the United Nations for the purpose of reviewing the present Charter may be held at a date and place to be fixed by a two-thirds vote of the members of the General Assembly and by a vote of any nine members of the Security Council. Each Member of the United Nations shall have one vote in the conference.

2. Any alteration of the present Charter recommended by a two-thirds vote of the conference shall take effect when ratified in accordance with their respective constitutional processes by two thirds of the Members of the United Nations including all the permanent members of the Security Council.

3. If such a conference has not been held before the tenth annual session of the General Assembly following the coming into force of the present Charter, the proposal to call such a conference shall be placed on the agenda of that session of the General Assembly, and the conference shall be held if so decided by a majority vote of the members of the General Assembly and by a vote of any nine members of the Security Council.

Chapter XXIX
AMENDMENTS

Article 182

Amendments to this Charter shall come into force for all Members of the United Nations when they have been adopted by a vote of two-thirds of the Members of the General Assembly and ratified in accordance with their respective constitutional processes by two-thirds of the Members of the United Nations, including three-fourths of the permanent Members of the Security Council, and the concurrence of the special permanent Members designated in Article 23.

Article 183

1. A General Conference of the Members of the United Nations for the purpose of reviewing this Charter may be held at a date and place to be fixed by a two-thirds vote of the Members of the General Assembly and by a vote of any twelve Members of the Security Council. Each Member of the United Nations shall have one vote in the conference.

2. Any alteration of the present Charter recommended by a two-thirds vote of the Conference shall take effect when ratified in accordance with their respective constitutional processes by two-thirds of the Members of the United Nations, including three-fourths of the permanent Members of the Security Council and the concurring votes of the special permanent Members.

3. If such a Conference has not been held before the twentieth annual session of the General Assembly following the coming into force of this Charter, the proposal to call such a conference shall be placed on the agenda of that session of the General Assembly, and the Conference shall be held if so decided by a majority vote of the Members of the General Assembly and by a vote of any twelve Members of the Security Council.

A General Conference for reviewing this Charter may be held at a date and place fixed by a two-thirds vote of the Members.

Chapter XIX
RATIFICATION AND SIGNATURE

Article 110

1. The present Charter shall be ratified by the signatory states in accordance with their respective constitutional processes.

2. The ratifications shall be deposited with the Government of the United States of America, which shall notify all the signatory states of each deposit as well as the Secretary-General of the Organization when he has been appointed.

3. The present Charter shall come into force upon the deposit of ratifications by the Republic of China, France, the Union of Soviet Socialist Republics, the United Kingdom of Great Britain and Northern Ireland, and the United States of America, and by a majority of the other signatory states. A protocol of the ratifications deposited shall thereupon be drawn up by the Government of the United States of America which shall communicate copies thereof to all the signatory states.

4. The states signatory to the present Charter which ratify it after it has come into force will become original Members of the United Nations on the date of the deposit of their respective ratifications.

Article 111

The present Charter, of which the Chinese, French, Russian, English, and Spanish texts are equally authentic, shall remain deposited in the archives of the Government of the United States of America. Duly certified copies thereof shall be transmitted by that Government to the Governments of the other signatory states.

IN FAITH WHEREOF the representatives of the Governments of the United Nations have signed the present Charter.

DONE at the city of San Francisco the twenty-sixth day of June, one thousand nine hundred and forty-five.

Chapter XXX
RATIFICATION AND SIGNATURE

Article 184

1. This Charter shall be ratified by the signatory states in accordance with their respective constitutional processes.

2. The ratification shall be deposited with the government of the United States of America, which shall notify all the signatory states of each deposit as well as the Secretary-General of the Organization when he or she has been appointed.

3. This Charter shall come into force upon the deposit of ratifications by the special permanent Members of the Security Council, by three-fourths of the other permanent Members of the Security Council, and by two-thirds of the Member states of the United Nations as organized under the preceding Charter signed on June 26, 1945. A protocol of the ratifications deposited shall thereupon be drawn up by the government of the United States of America that shall communicate copies thereof to all signatory states.

4. The additional signatories to this Charter who ratify it within one year after it comes into force will also become original Members of the United Nations, on the date of the deposit of their respective ratifications.

Article 185

This Charter, of which the Chinese, French, Russian, English, Spanish, and Arabic texts are equally authentic, shall remain deposited in the archives of the government of the United States of America. Duly certified copies thereof shall be transmitted by the government of the United States of America to the governments of the other signatory states.

IN FAITH WHEREOF, the representatives of the governments of the United Nations have signed this Charter on the _____ day of _____ in the year 19_____.
(SIGNATORIES)

This Charter shall be ratified by the signatory states in accordance with their respective constitutional processes.